THIS OLD
HARLEY

The Ultimate Tribute to the World's Greatest Motorcycle

Edited by
Michael Dregni

With stories, photographs, and artwork from
Evel Knievel, Arlen Ness, Peter Egan, Allan Girdler,
Harry V. Sucher, David K. Wright, Cook Neilson,
David Edwards, Melissa Holbrook Pierson,
James Guçwa, Dave Barnhouse, Roy Bacon,
Timothy Remus, Dr. Martin Jack Rosenblum,
Buzz Kanter, Lucky Lee Lott, Andrew Morland,
Jerry Irwin, Brian Blades, Nick Cedar, and more.

Inspiring | Educating | Creating | Entertaining

Brimming with creative inspiration, how-to projects, and useful information to enrich your everyday life, Quarto Knows is a favorite destination for those pursuing their interests and passions. Visit our site and dig deeper with our books into your area of interest: Quarto Creates, Quarto Cooks, Quarto Homes, Quarto Lives, Quarto Drives, Quarto Explores, Quarto Gifts, or Quarto Kids.

This edition published in 2017 by Crestline,
an imprint of The Quarto Group
142 West 36th Street, 4th Floor
New York, NY 10018 USA
T (212) 779-4972 F (212) 779-6058
www.QuartoKnows.com

Crestline titles are also available at discount for retail, wholesale, promotional, and bulk purchase. For details, contact the Special Sales Manager by mail at specialsales@quarto.com or by mail at The Quarto Group, Attn: Special Sales Manager, 401 Second Avenue North, Suite 310, Minneapolis, MN 55401 USA.

ISBN-13: 978-0-7858-3506-6

Editor: Michael Dregni
Design Manager: James Kegley
Layout Designer: Andrea Rud

Printed in China

10 9 8 7 6 5 4 3 2

Legal Notice
This Is not an official publication of Harley-Davidson. The name Harley-Davidson ® as well as certain names, model designation, and logo designs, are the property of H-D Michigan Inc. ("Harley-Davidson"). We use them for identification purposes only. Neither the author, photographer, publisher, nor this book is in any way affiliated with Harley-Davidson, Inc., or H-D Michigan Inc.

Permissions
Quarto Publishing Group USA Inc. have made every effort to determine original sources and locate copyright holders of the materials in this book. Please bring to our attention any errors of fact, omission, or copyright.

"The Perfect Vehicle" by Melissa Holbrook Pierson from *The Perfect Vehicle: What It Is About Motorcycles.* © 1997 Melissa Holbrook Pierson. Reprinted with permission of W. W. Norton & Company, Inc.

"Evel Ways" by Evel Knievel from *Evel Ways: A Daring Approach to Life the Attitude of Evel Knievel.* © 1999 GraF/X. Reprinted with permission of Scott Bachman and GraF/X Publishing Services.

On the cover: 1936 Model E Knucklehead. (Photograph © Randy Leffingwell)

On the frontis: A postcard to the folks back home from somewhere along Route 66, the Great American Highway. Elvis waves from his Harley KH. Poster for The Wild One. Easy Rider Billy Blake and Captain America replicas. Owner: Otis Chandler. (Photograph © Brian Blades/Cycle World)

On the title pages: A classic Harley rests in the shade. (Shutterstock)

Opposite the contents page: This 1963 Harley-Davidson FLH began life as a police bike. Owner Steve Barloggi restored it to "civilian" specifications, applied to new paint and wiring, and added factory FLH accessories from the period. (Photograph © Nick Cedar)

Acknowledgments

My thanks to everyone involved with this project, including in alphabetical order: Roy Bacon; Dave Barnhouse; Kent Bash; Keith Baum; Brian Blades; Rick Budd, Reynolds-Alberta Museum; Nick Cedar; David Edwards, *Cycle World* magazine; John Dean; Peter Egan; Ciara Fox; Allan Girdler; James "Kingneon" Guçwa; Suzanne Hunsinger, Curtis Publishing Company; Jerry Irwin; Buzz Kanter, *American Iron Magazine*; Evel and Kelly Knievel; Randy Leffingwell; Doug Leikala; Leslie Levy; Lucky Lee Lott of Hell Drivers fame; Andrew Morland; Cook Neilson; Arlen Ness and Timothy Remus; Melissa Holbrook Pierson; Dr. Martin Jack Rosenblum, Historian at Harley-Davidson, Inc.; Harry V. Sucher; Lowell Thompson, the Hadley Companies; and David K. Wright.

"Hell on wheels"
A Wall of Death advertising poster promises chills and spills—and the Angel of Death has front-row tickets.

Contents

This Old Harley

 Most of us who have motorcycles in our blood remember the first time we saw a Harley-Davidson. Harleys have a way of catching the eye—and often, of changing lives.

There's no easy explanation for this, except for the simple fact that Harley-Davidsons are not just motorcycles, even to the ordinary Joe or Jane. Harleys are an American icon revered 'around the globe. They're a household name, art on wheels, a fantasy in chrome, a full-throated declaration of independence, a poke in the eye to the status quo, an obsession, a religion, a way of life—as well as a machine backed by one of the best marketing campaigns in history.

Harley-Davidsons have been the ride of choice for Clark Gable and Elvis Presley, Brigitte Bardot and Elizabeth Taylor, Gene Vincent and Evel Knievel. Lee Marvin threw his leg over a Harley as the "bad" outlaw biker in *The Wild One*. Peter Fonda and Dennis Hopper set sail on chopped Harleys—former Los Angeles Police Department Panheads, ironically—in *Easy Rider*. If ever there was a legendary motorcycle, Harley-Davidson is it.

The events that led to the first time I saw a Harley could be painted by numbers into your typical Norman Rockwell–esque scene—but with a movie-script ending that you can probably already imagine.

It was long ago on one of those buzz-cut days of summers past. A buddy and I had set out on our Schwinn Stingrays on a fishing expedition, bamboo poles and a can of freshly dug worms in hand. We stopped by the local dairy store for a soda pop and a pack of baseball cards so we'd have something to do while we waited in hopes that a finny critter would actually bite.

"Bill and Wanda's"
Artist James "Kingneon" Guçwa's paintings of Harleys are chock full of brilliant colors and neon lights, creating a larger-than-legend image of the machines. "Bill and Wanda's" was done with oil paints on canvas. (Painting © 1998/Courtesy of Leslie Levy Creative Art Licensing)

The Harley was there in the dairy-store parking lot, leaning over at a jaunty, cool angle on its kickstand. The chrome gleamed in the summer sun, casting off rays of reflected light that—at least in my memory now—made me shield my eyes as if a halo encircled the machine. It was all dressed up with a world of places to go. The engine was right there out in the open, bare naked and apologizing for nothing. The long chrome pipes shined like they didn't care who knew how beautiful they were. The cycle had floorboards as large as the running boards on our family's Volkswagen Bug, whitewall tires like a T-bucket hot rod, a windscreen splattered with dead bugs from roads since traveled. The machine was long and wide and big. It was straddled by saddlebags straight off Roy Rogers's Trigger. It had the muscles of Charles Atlas from a comic-book ad. It was a rocketship on wheels that would make Buck Rogers green with envy. Standing there on a summer day, we could feel the heat the engine gave off. A small splotch of hot oil steamed where it had soiled the blacktop, like a hack of chewing tobacco from a baseball star.

Then the door of the dairy store swung open, and a young guy dressed in blue jeans and black leather came striding out like a modern-day cowboy. He looked at my friend and me staring at his ride and smiled a toothy all-American grin as he swung his leg over the bike.

"Hey guys," he said.

We were too amazed to even answer.

With a push of a button, the bike came to life. The rider smiled at us again and then wheeled the cycle backwards in that strange, crablike walk. With a clunk, he shifted into gear and roared off down the street and into the sunset.

I was hooked like a sunfish on the end of the line of my bamboo pole.

For most of us, time could be divided into the years before our first Harley encounter and those after. Suddenly, everything in the world looked different.

Many of the stories, tall tales, essays, and reminiscences in this anthology tell of that first Harley in one way or another. The authors include two world-famous motorcycle daredevils, one world-renowned customizer, a couple of racers, a bunch of well-known magazine writers and book authors, Harley-Davidson's own official historian and archivist, and several ordinary folk who simply love Harleys and have a good yarn to tell.

If you are still in awe of that first Harley, still riding and wrenching on Harleys, or still dreaming of Harleys, then this book is for you.

Michael Dregni

1954 Harley-Davidson FL

Elvis Presley owned an FL, and you couldn't ask for a better endorsement than that. The Motor Company's Big Twins of the 1950s and 1960s were true Cadillacs for the working class. Adorned with a glowing paint scheme, dressed up by saddle bags and a luxurious seat, and jeweled with chrome, the 74-ci (1,212-cc) FL was the epitome of American motorcycling in its day. Owner: Ben Yarschenko. (Photograph © John Dean/Reynolds-Alberta Museum)

Chapter 1

In the Beginning . . .

*"I pity the poor people who don't
ride motorcycles."*
—Malcolm Smith, champion motorcycle racer

Whether it was a Topper or an Electra-Glide, most of us look back fondly on our first motorcycle. Sometimes, too fondly.

Often our memories have become selective: We remember the rare times our first cycle actually ran and have largely forgotten about the hours spent trying to make sense of the spider's web that was supposed to be a vintage wiring harness. Brakes that broke, switches that didn't turn things on or off, suspension that didn't suspend, engine cases and gaskets that failed to keep oil inside—years later, we all look back on these woes of our first machines and laugh.

That's the magic of a first motorcycle.

Another happy owner, 1928
With handshake ablur, another happy owner takes possession of his new Harley-Davidson from his friendly neighborhood dealer. This wasn't just any motorcycling enthusiast, however: The new owner here was none other than aviator Speed Holman, winner of the 1927 National Air Races. Speed was shaking hands with Minneapolis, Minnesota, dealer George Faulders after taking possession of his new Model 28.

The Bike in the Barn, or, What My Folks Didn't Know, Didn't Hurt . . . Me

By Allan Girdler

Allan Girdler has probably logged more miles on a Harley XR-750 than just about anyone. Although Jay Springsteen might beat him around a half-mile dirttrack, and Ricky Graham probably has more race jewelry on display in his den, Allan has vintage-raced his own iron XR-750 for years—and even *toured* on it for goodness sakes.

Allan is a former editor of *Car Life* and *Cycle World* magazines as well as an executive editor of *Road & Track*. He is also the author of an eclectic blend of books on motoring history, from his well-known *Harley-Davidson: The American Motorcycle*, *Harley Racers*, *The Harley-Davidson and Indian Wars*, *Illustrated Harley-Davidson Buyer's Guide*, and *Harley-Davidson XR-750* to tomes on NASCAR and sports-racing specials.

His fascination with motorcycles had humble beginnings, however, as he relates in this classic tale of a bike found in a barn.

When I first sat down to recount—better make that confess—how I got my first motorcycle, taught myself to ride, and didn't tell my folks what I was up to, I thought, Gee, maybe I'd better put in something along the lines of "Kids, don't try this at home."

And then I thought, Naw, history tells us that Gottleib Daimler, builder of the first gas-powered motorcycle, waited until his wife was away before that machine's first test, proving to me at least that if we waited for parental permission or approval, there wouldn't be any motorcycles.

So, kids of all ages, I'm not telling you to try this at home, all I'm saying is I did it, I got away with it, my life has never been the same, and I'm glad I did it.

What I did began the summer I was seventeen, with a call from my best friend, also seventeen and also lacking in common sense. Our mutual interest was in finding derelict Fords, hauling them home and souping them up.

He'd been reading the classifieds and found an ad for a 1934 Harley-Davidson and he wanted me to come help him look at it.

I'd admired motorcycles from a distance and once crashed my cousin's motor scooter into a hedge when I swerved to avoid a passing police car, but my mo-

Tike and his new bike, 1950s

After clambering aboard a Harley-Davidson Model S 125, the world was a new place full of wonder—and there's no looking back. The look on Junior's face here says it all.

torcycle knowledge totaled zero, same as his. Seemed to me that two times nothing is nothing, as the song says, but I was game to look and learn.

The seller was a couple of years older than us and vastly experienced. He gave us a short tour, as in "That's the clutch, that's the gearshift, that's the front brake, and that's the throttle," and he clearly figured that was all we needed to know.

We figured the same. When I say now that the 1934 Harley-Davidson had a foot clutch and hand shift, it sounds odd if not impossible. But Harleys, and Indians, used the system until after World War II and although new bikes had hand clutches and foot shifts when we paid this visit, we didn't know that 'cause we didn't know anything about motor-cycles.

How little? My pal swung a leg over the bike, unfolded the kick lever, reared up in the air, and gave a mighty heave down.

It hadn't occurred to him that the bike might be in gear, which of course it was. And for the only time in our acquaintance, the old Harley fired on the first kick.

It had been parked in the garage, facing in, and when the engine caught the bike leaped forward, climbed the garage's back wall, and described a perfect half gainer, straight up, then arcing gracefully over and down.

My pal had thoughtfully placed himself between the falling motorcycle and the garage floor, so the bike wasn't damaged.

He was bruised, scraped, and completely unin-terested in learning any more about motorcycles.

I was enthralled. I thought this motorcycle was the most wonderful device I'd ever seen, so I anted up the asking price of $50—oh, wait a bit.

Might be useful here to pause for another expla-nation. When people hear I bought a classic old an-tique Harley-Davidson for pocket change, they as-sume that I was smarter than other people, getting this wonderful classic for next to nothing, and they usually wonder, do I regret not having kept it?

No. I didn't buy a collectible antique. What I bought was a clapped-out piece of old iron that no-body else wanted, which is why it was so cheap.

This occurred so long ago, 1954 if you need to know, that not only was nostalgia not as good then

as it is now, nostalgia hadn't been invented yet.

What we've done since is shift our focus, so nowa-days the folks with too much money are buying old Harleys and the kids with no money are buying ob-solete motocross bikes for $50 and learning the hard way how they work.

Which is exactly what I did back then, wobbling home on a motorcycle older than me, stalling the engine and grinding gears until I learned how to co-ordinate the controls.

That was the easy part.

The part I really had trouble with was, I didn't have to ask to know what mom and dad would say to a motorcycle. My folks came of age in hard times. They were not, as we say now, risk-takers. They didn't have to know even as much as I did to know there were reasons people spoke of murdercycles.

(Years and years later, my dad admitted that his uncle Pat—the family daredevil and, I surmised, ne'er-do-well—rode an Indian. But this wasn't some-thing said in public or when children were present.)

But by happy chance one of my brothers hoped to ride rodeo and he kept his cutting horse in a re-mote barn up the road, so that's where I put the Harley. There was enough space for me and my broth-ers to practice starts and stops and riding in circles: One of my treasured childhood images is my younger brother rising into the air above the machine, de-scribing a graceful arc and landing, head-first, in front of the front wheel. The old 74 had quite a kick when you neglected, as my brother had, to retard the spark before leaping on the start lever.

And I ventured out on the open road. I did have a driver's license and I sort of think now there was no motorcycle requirement in my home state then. And the Harley was registered, albeit not to me: I was a minor, after all. Nor did the thought of insur-ance trouble me. I simply didn't have any.

Oh, one reason I never found out about the legal concerns was that I never got stopped, and I never got stopped I think now because I wasn't wearing a helmet—kids, don't pay attention to this part—and I didn't get stopped because all the cops in that part of the state knew me, because when I was sixteen I looked twelve and when I first got my license I was stopped thirty times in the first thirty-one days I went public with my old Ford, which had lots of carbure-

1934 Harley-Davidson VLD

Above: *The Motor Company's dazzling new V Series made its auspicious debut as 1930 models. Gone were the venerable F-head Big Twins, and in their place were the stunning new side-valve V Series models. The dramatic change in valvetrain configuration was nothing less than a revolution, as the F-head design had been a Harley-Davidson mainstay for decades. Owner: Steve Slocombe. (Photograph © Andrew Morland)*

1967 Harley-Davidson FLH Electra-Glide

Above: *Some kids never get that first Harley out of the blood. Albert Remme bought this Electra-Glide brand spanking new in 1967 and has owned it ever since. Remme is a farmer and lives at the end of a long dirt road, so every time he goes out for a ride, his pride and joy gets suited in dirt or mud. He painstakingly cleans it after every excursion, keeping the old machine in beautiful condition even today. Working his farm, however, he has too little time to tour, so his FLH boasts only 28,000 miles. (Photograph © Andrew Morland)*

"American Made"

Overleaf: *Almost every motorcyclist remembers the first time they saw a Harley—and it was often in such a setting, parked in front of the local store. Artist Dave Barnhouse's images of Harley-Davidson motorcycles are pure nostalgia. With their warm colors and golden lighting, they are a road trip straight down memory lane. (the Hadley Companies)*

tors, exhaust pipes sticking out the side, no hood, no top, and no fenders. The police must have figured it was just that loopy kid doing another dumb thing, which of course I was doing. They simply didn't know the degree of dumb, is all.

I had two partners in this foolishness. One was the errant son of an old-money family, whose name you'd recognize if I gave it, which I won't because ratting on pals isn't done in my circle. He had an Indian older than my Harley. The second bike nut was a kid from the docks, who'd quit school and made enough to buy a new Harley-Davidson, the sports model, painted bright red.

Thank goodness.

The thanks are because there I was, rumbling down the only road through our little town when I passed . . . Grandma.

Gulp. As it happened, Grandma was cool, I mean she drove a Barracuda, no kidding. But she was still Grandma and she looked at me and I waved—put on a bold face, I told myself—and she waved back.

She got home before I did, which I know because Mom was at the door.

"Grandma says you passed her, on a big, red motorcycle."

"Oh yeah," I said as the perfect fib occurred to me, "I was on Rocky's bike. I wanted to learn how."

Rocky was a member of the Fix Or Repair Daily Club, so Mom had seen his motorcycle, which was undeniably red, so she delivered Safety Lecture #4, and that was that.

And anyway, I did want to learn how, which I did. Tipped over some but didn't crash, I think now because I was so intimated I didn't take the chances that lead to disaster.

When the registration expired, though, the fun stopped. I knew that would be noticed and I'd be stopped and

Harley-Davidson Topper
Below: *On the heels of the successful American Cushman and world-changing Italian Vespa scooters, the Motor Company hopped on the bandwagon with its Topper. Harley's scooter was kind of a Hell's Angels starter cycle, a putt-putt version of a Panhead with training wheels for Junior and Sis. It was draped in angular two-tone fiberglass bodywork and started by a crude pull-start borrowed from an outboard motor. Unfortunately, Harley entered the scooter market just as the fad was fading, and the Topper never sold as well as was hoped. Owner: Ken Lee. (Photograph © Andrew Morland)*

my goose would be Christmas dinner. I gave the old Harley, still working well, to another pal and what happened to the machine after that, I don't know.

Years and years later I had occasion to ride an Indian from the era of my first Harley, as in foot clutch, hand shift, brakes engineered to not stop you without a lot of warning first, and I thought, This is impossible.

How lucky I was to not have known how tough it was, back then, 'cause if I'd known it was this difficult, I wouldn't have tried it.

And I would have missed the best part.

1939 Harley-Davidson 61 OHV Model EL
The Knucklehead was the machine everyone dreamed of owning. The "Knucklehead" moniker came from the shape of the aluminum-alloy rocker boxes that crowned Harley's fabulous new overhead-valve V-twin when it debuted in 1935. The 61 OHV was first available as the 61-ci (1,000-cc) Models E and high-compression EL Sportster. In 1941, the Motor Company bowed to demand from police departments for more power and introduced the 74-ci (1,212-cc) Models F and FL. Owner: Eldon Brown. (Photograph © John Dean/Reynolds-Alberta Museum)

Dressed for success

A Harley as it came from the dealer's showroom was simply a blank canvas on which the owner could create a masterpiece. Harley knew the drill here and offered a full line of accessories, speed gear, touring kits, and chrome trinkets so owners could dress their cycles for success. Memorabilia owner: Doug Leikala. (Photograph © Nick Cedar)

> *"It begins here for me on this road. How the whole mess happened, I don't know. But I know it couldn't happen again in a million years. Maybe I could have stopped it early. But once the trouble was on its way, I was just going with it. . . . This is where it begins for me, right on this road."*
> —Introduction to *The Wild One,* 1953

"Be Honest, Fair, and Never Give Up"

By Doug Leikala

Well, it all started way back in the early 1960s. Just like everyone else, I was riding mini bikes, Whizzers, and many other brands of motorcycles. My first Harley was a 1962 or 1963 Sprint. I don't remember if it was a C or H model. The bike wasn't in the best of shape when I got it to begin with. After some work to get it running, off I went.

In our neighborhood we had a large wooded area behind our local school. A lot of the older riders in the area had all kinds of trails and a short track already cut out. Me being about thirteen or fourteen, I got on the Sprint and headed out for the woods by myself. Well, it wasn't long and I was an expert trail rider—or so I thought. Somehow after going over jumps and up and down hills the motor guard on the bottom of the bike must have come loose and dropped down. I caught a tree root going down a hill, and the bike suddenly came to a halt and I went over the bars. As I rolled down the hill, the bike passed me up, also in an end-over-end roll. I stopped, the bike stopped, and when I got over to the bike, the front forks and bars were bent so much the bike couldn't be ridden. I left it there and walked home. The next day, my older brother and I went to get the bike and it was gone. I never did see it again.

That did not stop me, as my collection has grown to many Harleys from 1910 to 1999. I started collecting in 1974 and opened my shop the same year. I have maybe the largest memorabilia collection in the United States, possibly the world. The collection ranges from the bikes themselves to pins, fobs, buttons, clothing, postcards, matchbook covers, stamps, literature, signs, clocks, paint cans, oil cans, toys, etc. I've had the opportunity to have my collection appear in the local newspaper, different motorcycle trade journals, and two publications, one being *Harley-Davidson Collectibles* published by Voyageur Press.

My latest Harley-Davidson is a new 1999 Ultra Classic Twin Cam 88. Talk about a motorcycle with power to spare. My last new bike was a 1979 80 ci. But the most dear to my heart is my 1910 Harley-Davidson. One hundred percent original paint, decals, tires, and it's a very rare 26-inch model.

The 1910 came from southern Ohio. My wife and I went down to Kentucky to look at a 1913 that was to be all original. I took my sales literature for 1912, 1913, and 1914 so I could compare parts if it was a parts bike. When we got out of the car and into the gentleman's garage, I knew it was not a true 1913. I took out my literature and he asked me what I was doing. I told him the bike was a parts bike. Man, did he get mad. He told us to leave and the bike wasn't for sale.

So we headed back to Ohio. I told my wife about the 1910 around Cincinnati. We stopped to call and made arrangements to go and see the 1910. The bike was shoved between the garage and an old car; the cycle was covered up with only the back end showing. All I got was a peek of the back end of the bike. I asked if it was for sale and he said, "No." We left and I started my phone calls every couple months or so. I sent Christmas cards, found out his and his wife's birthday and sent birthday cards, and stopped down many times. Finally it paid off. He called me after three years of trying, and the bike now sits in my collection. So a word to any new or old collector. Be honest, fair, and never give up.

"No Motorcycles Allowed"

By Arlen Ness with Timothy Remus

Arlen Ness is *the* name in custom motorcycles. From humble beginnings painting gas tanks in the evening hours after his day job, Arlen has become the best-known Harley artist wherever customs are spoken of anywhere around the globe. Whether it's the bend of a set of bars, the sculpted line of a tank, or the style and color of his paintwork, he has something special, an eye for customizing motorcycles that many others can emulate but few can equal.

Arlen is also a gracious man. He's friendly and approachable on the streets of Daytona Beach or Sturgis, ready to share ideas or check out your own ride.

Surprisingly, for the man who would make his name with cycles, Arlen grew up in a household with the strict rule "No Motorcycles Allowed," as he relates here.

Though it seems hard to believe, I grew up without any motorcycles. It was my father who established the "No Motorcycles" rule, which meant that most of my early vehicles were cars instead of cycles.

The one exception was a certain Cushman scooter that I brought home during my early high school years. I don't think I was ever off that scooter. I didn't have a permit yet, so I had to stay close to home. I rode it around the block hundreds and hundreds of times each day. I must have worn a groove in the concrete in front of the house I rode that scooter around so much.

It had a body and a two-speed transmission. The shifter was keyed to its shaft and I was always shearing that key. Of course we didn't have the right key, so we would cut a small washer in half with the hacksaw and use that for a key. That would work for about a day's riding and then the key would shear again and the whole thing started over.

Before I was old enough to get a permit to ride the scooter legally, my Dad made me sell it and he never would let me buy a real motorcycle.

Later, in high school, I started buying cars and fixing those up. I had a '51 Merc that was pretty cool. Then I sold that and bought a T-Bucket. I put a Caddy engine in the T-bucket and painted it orange.

Arlen Ness Knucklehead

"In those days I didn't have enough money to just go out and buy another bike to customize. So I kept working on the Knucklehead," Arlen Ness recounted. The current version of Arlen's first bike uses a 19-inch (47.5-cm) front tire, twin front calipers, and fork tubes that plumb the master cylinder to the calipers. Bob Munroe built the hand-fabbed gas tank, which also incorporates a hidden oil tank. Frame tubes route oil to the engine, which displaces 100 ci (1,638 cc) thanks to stroker flywheels and oversize pistons. A #80 Magnuson blower, driven 1:1 by the crank, feeds the two Weber carburetors. By using the Sporty tranny, Arlen was able to have a huge Knucklehead engine with electric starting! The engraving was done on silver plate, which was then inlaid with gold and riveted to the engine and cases. Jeff McCann applied the paint with faces created by Dick DeBenedictis. (Photograph © Timothy Remus)

This was the mid-sixties, and on weekends I did a lot of cruising in the T-bucket. East 14th Street was the place to be, you spent your time going from drive-in to drive-in. The motorcycle guys hung out at The Quarter Pound and I drove by it all the time just to see the bikes. At the time I didn't know a Harley from a BSA, but the ones I liked had that low-slung look. Those turned out to be Harleys, of course, and I wanted one. Heck, I wanted one all the way back in high school but I could never have one. When I got married, Bev said she would never be married to a guy who rode a motorcycle. In those days a lot of the guys who rode were outlaws and she just didn't want me riding with them.

At this time, I was driving a truck delivering furniture. Each week I would save a few bucks out of my paycheck—I kept that money stashed in the back of my wallet in case a good deal came up on a bike. There was this cement factory in Oakland that I drove by sometimes when I was doing deliveries and there were always a couple of pretty nice Harleys parked there. Sometimes I went out of my way just to drive by and have another look at those bikes. One day there was a for-sale sign on one of the Harleys at the cement plant. The bike was 300 bucks and that's about how much I had saved in the back of my wallet.

I still didn't know anything about them at all, but an old friend from high school had a Harley. He went with me to look over the bike and said it was OK, so I did the deal. This Knucklehead had a suicide clutch and I didn't really know how to ride yet so my friend rode it to his house for me. He lived a mile from my house and I had to ride it the rest of the way home. I bet I killed it a thousand times between his place and mine. Finally, I pulled it up at my house and rapped the pipes, Bev opened the door, saw me on the bike and slammed the door.

"Across America"

From the time when he could first pick up a pencil, artist Kent Bash has been drawing pictures of Harley-Davidson cycles and hot-rodded cars. This image was created with oil paints on canvas. (Painting © Kent Bash)

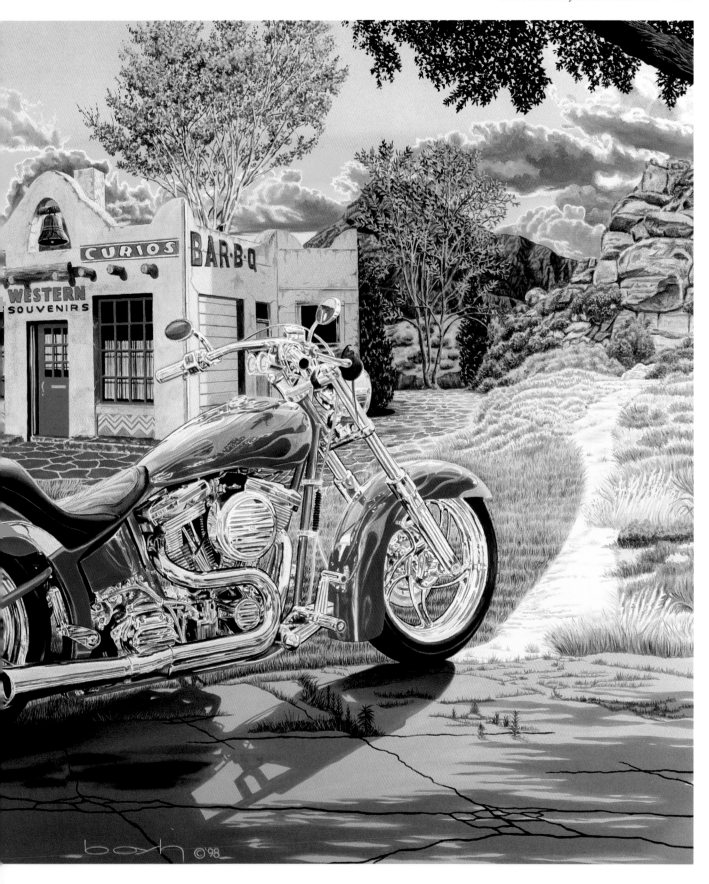

Mallard Teal Custom

Painter, designer, and builder Mallard Teal created this custom based on a 1987 FXLRC. Among the select parts are an Andrews transmission, Barnet clutch, Fournales air shocks, and GMA brakes. Mikuni carburetors feed fuel to the engine with a shot of nitrous oxide. Owner: Mallard Teal. (Photograph © Andrew Morland)

I did learn to ride it, and then I met other guys with bikes and rode with them. At the time I bought that first bike I already knew how to paint, so I put on a peanut tank and painted the Knucklehead right away. I put on some different bars too, but there really wasn't much stuff available in those days.

Once I painted the Knucklehead, other guys asked me to paint their bikes. I painted motorcycles part time for almost two years and pretty soon I had a lot of paint work, but I was still driving the truck delivering furniture during the day. I painted after my regular job and on Sundays and still couldn't get

all the work done. I eventually decided I didn't have enough time to do the painting so I quit driving furniture and started working as a carpenter. That way I had more free time because we worked four and a half days a week with days off whenever it rained. I did that for about six months.

Finally, I quit the carpenter's job and began just working at home full time. It was a big deal to do this because I already had a wife and two kids. Then the problem was my place became a hangout. Whenever one of the guys had a day off he came over with a six pack. So I didn't make any money that way because I didn't get any work done. That's why I rented the store, the little one on East 14th Street in San Leandro. It was open from 6 to 11 P.M., and people could see me there, so I wasn't bothered at home and got more work done that way. Then I started making parts. The ramhorn handlebars, for example, were one of my own products and they sold very well. Eventually we added tires and learned more about business at the same time.

In those days I didn't have enough money to just go out and buy another bike to customize. So I kept working on the Knucklehead. The third time I built that bike I made a sissy bar and a set of up-swept pipes. The rear fender came from an automotive continental kit and I put on a 21-inch front wheel. That was just coming into style at the time. The Avon was hard to get, so if you had a 21, you had a pretty cool bike.

Later, when I learned more about motors, I added the supercharger and grafted a Sportster transmission onto the back of the Big Twin engine. Nobody was doing work like that at the time. Eventually I got together enough money to buy a wrecked Sportster, which I fixed up and sold, and then I could start buying and selling a few bikes.

But I always kept the Knuckle and I'm really glad now that I did, because not very many guys still own their first Harley.

Harley-Davidson Custom

Below: *Arlen Ness's aftermarket custom parts are famous around the globe—witness this English Harley that has been customized with well-chosen parts from Ness's catalog. Dressed in purple paint, this Softail frame houses a 1,340-cc engine. Owner: Bernie Stafford. (Photograph © Andrew Morland)*

"Tattoo Wayne" Custom

Drag racer "Tattoo Wayne" Loftain built this dresser with attitude. The engine is a 110-ci (1,802-cc) S&S V-Twin with S&S 10.8:1 heads by Baisley, an S&S cam, and an S&S "D" carburetor that fathers 121 rear-wheel hp on the dyno and 120 lb-ft of torque. Wayne lowered the bike about 2 inches and added the rake to the fork neck. The fairing is by Bob Drone, the rear fender from Arlen Ness, and the front fender from Jesse James. (Photograph © Timothy Remus)

Arlen Ness 1957 Chevy Custom

Arlen crafted this cycle in about 1996. The design was drawn by Carl Brouhard and the metal worked by Ron Covell. All of the chrome trim on the tailfins and the rear taillight treatment were formed by hand. The engine is a Ness V-Twin with full billet treatment. (Photograph © Timothy Remus)

"Denver Arlin" Custom

Arlin Fatland, longtime owner of The Two Wheelers Shop in Denver, Colorado, crafted this retro ride. "We tried to make it look like an old FL with styling cues from an old hot rod I saw a while back," explained Arlin. Though the frame is stock, the bike has a certain mass you don't see on most Sportsters. Part of the bike's bulk is provided by the 16-inch (40-cm) tires, part of it is the Wide-Glide fork assembly, and part is the extended tank and full-wrap rear fender. Bikes built in the days of the bobbers and early flathead hot rods featured limited chrome due simply to the expense of chrome plating. Thus, Arlin chose to have the 16-inch (40-cm) rims powder-coated red and fitted with period-look whitewalls. (Photograph © Timothy Remus)

Over-Customized Harleys

There's a fine point at which art no longer imitates life, but where art initiates life, becoming an entirely new entity. These "over-customized" Harleys poke fun at motorcycling, customized machines, and art itself.

Long pipes save lives
Right: *Extra-lengthy mufflers trumpet the sound of this over-customized Harley. (Photograph © Jerry Irwin)*

Mystery machine
Below, left: *Almost every surface of this Harley is covered in painted graphics, metal castings, or engravings. (Photograph © Jerry Irwin)*

One-cycle parade
Below, right: *Exactly 1,400 lights illuminate the road for this custom. (Photograph © Andrew Morland)*

Bison-Glide

Dressed in buffalo hide, this Harley is ready for the stampede to Sturgis. (Photograph © Keith Baum)

Pretty in pink

This pink Softail is accessorized with white saddlebags and plenty of fringe. (Photograph © Keith Baum)

Ratbike

A prime example of a long lineage of ratted-out cycles. (Photograph © Jerry Irwin)

First Harley

By Peter Egan

Peter Egan has become a sort of garage prophet of motorcyclists. He is equal parts sage and common man, imparting wisdom from the school of hard knocks and relating tales of motorcycling culture chock full of universal truths.

As a columnist and writer for *Cycle World* magazine, Peter Egan boasts one of the best deals going: He actually gets paid to ride motorcycles. In fact, Peter's columns for both *Cycle World* and *Road & Track* are the favorite reads of many two- and four-wheeled enthusiasts, at times garnering more mail in both magazines than the rest of the editorial content combined.

From Triumphs to Ducatis, BMWs to Vincents, Peter is enamored with a wide array of makes and models of cycles beyond Harley-Davidson. In this reminiscence, however, he chronicles the circumstances that led him to the Milwaukee fold.

My first Harley? Well, I confess that I did not buy a Harley-Davidson from an actual dealer until 1990, when the product had been made safe from catastrophic mechanical failure by the arrival of the Evolution engine and a decade of hard work by Harley engineers, who strove earnestly to improve quality.

I bought a 1990 883 Sportster, brand new, from a local dealer, then moved up to a 1994 Electra-Glide Sport, which got bartered into an emerald-green 1998 Road King. So I am a latecomer to H-D ownership, but not to Harley exposure.

In truth, the first motorcycles I ever saw, rode upon, and *tried* to buy were all Harleys, right from the early fifties onward. Let me explain.

When my parents moved our family from St. Paul, Minnesota, to the small Wisconsin town of Elroy (pop. 1,503) in 1952, we temporarily rented the upstairs of a house from a widow and her son, Buford. Buford had just returned, unscathed, from the Korean War and belonged to that slightly sullen, restless, pre-rock 'n' roll generation of rebels who felt something was not quite right in their lives, but didn't know what. Maybe it was the H-bomb threat, or the inexplicable cancer of world Communism and the bleak, unromantic police work needed to contain it.

In any case, Buford had a Harley-Davidson, which he parked just outside our back stairs. I was only four at the time and didn't know one motorcycle from another, but this one was no doubt a full-boat Panhead, which I remember as having leather saddlebags and a large, sprung buddy seat, all with more conchos than the Cisco Kid's saddle and gunbelt put together. It also had a full windshield with a Vicks-bottle blue lower half, a tank-shift knob, and tires as big as something off a car.

Buford and his mother used to argue a lot about his motorcycle, the late hours he kept, and his bad friends. When this happened, Buford would slam the

"Tex"
Like moths drawn to a candle, these impressionable youths were goners. After seeing their reflection in the chrome, collecting baseball cards was no longer good enough. Artist Stevan Dohanos painted this image that graced the cover of the Saturday Evening Post *on April 7, 1951. (Courtesy the Curtis Publishing Company)*

back door, climb on the motorcycle, give it a mighty kick, set his black sea-captain's hat just so on his head, light a cigarette, and bellow off down the street, with the cigarette sparkling like a firecracker fuse. His mother would stand on the back stoop, shouting until he was out of sight.

When he returned in the wee hours of the morning, she would reappear on the back stoop like a mechanical *glockenspiel* figure and resume shouting where she'd left off.

Sometimes Buford's mother visited our upstairs apartment and complained about her son to my mother. She would turn her head to one side, scuff her hands off one another like someone playing the cymbals, and moan, "Ohhh, Buford and them *motor-sickles!*"

I was naturally drawn to the excitement of the big Harley (and the miracle of human balance it required), and I spent a lot of time gazing at the bike and watching Buford work on it in his dungarees, engineer boots, and white T-shirt.

One day while I was doing this, I told Buford I really liked his motorcycle. He nodded, and then—as if suddenly struck by a terrible thought—he crouched down, grabbed me by the shoulders, and looked into my face. He squinted at me with one eye (the other one forced closed by smoke streaming upward from his ever-present Lucky Strike) and said fiercely, "Don't ever buy an Indian! Buy a Harley."

I assured him I wouldn't.

As it turned out, the Indian factory went out of business the next year, when I was five years old, so the temptation never materialized.

In fact, I managed to get through the entire decade without so much as a ride on a motorcycle—or a two-wheeled vehicle of any kind. But in 1961 my luck finally changed.

At thirteen, I had become a certified car nut and used to spend my Saturdays hitch-hiking to junkyards all over the county so I could sit in old cars and look at them and assess their street-rod and stock-car potential. I was doing this one fine autumn weekend, standing by the side of Highway 80 between Elroy and New Lisbon, Wisconsin, with my thumb out, trying to bum a ride to a New Lisbon wrecking yard.

Suddenly, a couple of full-dress Harleys roared

by and, to my amazement, immediately pulled over and stopped. Or at least one of them did. The other guy took longer to slow down and stop. He wasn't sure it was such a good idea.

"What are you doing?" he said, looking back at his buddy with a pained expression.

"Come on," his pal said, "let's give the kid a ride."

Both guys lit cigarettes (which at that time virtually everyone did during any brief moment of pause) and the friendly one slid forward on his fringed buddy seat and said, "Hop on, kid." He tilted his cap just right, gunned the big Panhead a few times, and we were off.

On the way to New Lisbon I looked over his shoulder, with tears streaming from my eyes in the wind, and saw we were doing an indicated 80 mph on the big round speedometer in the middle of his gas tank. I looked around myself at the passing landscape as we sped down the road and thought, *This is the finest moment of my life; the best thing I've ever done.*

By the time we got to New Lisbon, I was a goner. If these two guys had told me they were going to Denver or California, I would have said "That's exactly where I'm going," and faced the consequences later. (Hi, Mom? Is this you? I'm at a phone booth in North Platte. Listen, I just had to *ride. . . .*")

Fortunately, they were only going to the Harley dealer in New Lisbon, a small shop at the south edge of town. By the time we got there, I didn't want to go to the junkyard any more; I just wanted to be in a shop where motorcycles could be found. Some idling gear in my brain had rotated into position and positively engaged the concept of owning my own motorcycle, the sooner the better.

I spent the rest of the afternoon hanging around in the shadows of the dark, greasy shop as inconspicuously as possible, listening to the talk, looking at bikes, absorbing information, checking out piles of dusty parts, and watching half-disassembled gearboxes and engines drool 60-weight oil into cakepans and sawdust.

It was a whole new world, discovering the engine room of your ship, whose massive crankshaft and pistons made it possible to ply the open seas and travel anywhere on earth. One was immediately connected to the other and they couldn't be separated. Not at that time, anyway. Motorcyclists were mechanics.

1962 Harley-Davidson 165 Ranger

Ray Wesser was a well-known American Motorcyclist Association (AMA) district referee in northern California in the late 1940s and early 1950s. He eventually became a district sales manager for Harley after meeting Walter Davidson Jr. in 1953. He covered California, Oregon, and Washington in a job he held for twenty-five years. Ray and other dealers asked the Motor Company to configure a lightweight bike for trail use; the Ranger was the result. This Ranger was one of Ray's demonstrators, which he liked so much that he later bought it and has kept it ever since for trail riding and fishing trips. (Photograph © Nick Cedar)

This would change when Japanese bikes began to arrive in some numbers a few years later, but in 1961 I was visiting the last of the old-time motorcycle shops, undisturbed by progress, "the nicest people," or my own generation's coming of age.

I visited the shop many times after that, and in 1963 I saw an old Harley for sale at a gas station in the nearby village of Union Center. It was a battered 45-inch flathead, a WLA war surplus Army bike that had been repainted in a kind of dull primer red. Ev-

erything was red—wheels, spokes, tank, even the sidewalls of the tires. A sloppy spray-can job. But it was a real Harley, and it ran. Or so I was told. The gas station owner wanted $100 for it.

He started it up and I took my first ever motorcycle ride. I was too young (fifteen) to take it on the highway, so I rode down a gravel farm road and did a big lap around a nearby cow pasture. Surprisingly, I was able to operate the foot clutch, hand throttle and tank shift okay (hours and hours of imaginary

practice), but had a moment of hesitation with the brakes and ran into a couple of empty oil drums behind the gas station and fell over on the bike's crashbars.

No damage was done and I got the Harley back on its wheels just as the owner—who was building a stock car—came running around the corner with a welding mask tipped up on his head. "What was all that noise?"

"Nothing. I just bumped into an oil drum."

He glared at me uneasily.

I told him I'd buy the bike, and went home to get my meager savings out of the bank and then to sell my .410 shotgun and the Briggs & Stratton-powered mini bike I'd built. Within a couple of weeks, I had the hundred dollars and returned to the gas station.

"I've changed my mind," the man said, without looking up from his work. "I'm going to keep the Harley."

And that was the end of attempted Harley ownership for another twenty-seven years. Instead of the Harley 45, I bought a little Bridgestone 50 Sport, brand new, from the local hardware store. From 45 cubic inches (750 cc) to 50 cc displacement, in one fell swoop. After that, I worked my way upward through a series of Hondas, Triumphs, Nortons, Ducatis, etc.

A friend once said to me, "Your life might have been quite different if you'd bought that Harley instead of the Bridgestone 50. You might have had different experiences, a different outlook, completely different friends . . . "

I don't know how much of that is true. Our friends are our friends. But the open road might have been a lot more inviting—at least in my imagination—on a big Harley than it was on that Bridgestone 50 with its shoulder-hugging top speed of 37 mph. I might have gone to Denver, or even California instead of just buzzing around town and visiting my pals on nearby farms. Maybe the difference between Jack Kerouac and the rest of us was only a sense of scale, or picking the right first bike.

Youths led astray, 1950s

Left: *Hanging around the local Harley-Davidson dealership led many a youth happily astray. These two youngsters were doing their homework at Karl's Cycles in Minneapolis, Minnesota, a landmark for local riders for decades. (Minnesota Historical Society)*

"The Drifter"

Overleaf: *Just the kind of influences your Ma and Pa warned you about: motorcycles and that new music, rock 'n' roll. Artist James "Kingneon" Guçwa used acrylic paints on canvas in crafting this image. (Painting © 1999/Courtesy of Leslie Levy Creative Art Licensing)*

1996 Harley-Davidson Buell Lightning

Above: *Erik Buell must have sometimes felt like a fish out of water. He was a Harley-Davidson engineer with a taste for sporting motorcycles, which seemed like a dramatic contradiction as Harley-Davidson had a corner on the North American cruiser market. At the dawn of the 1980s, Buell left Harley and set up his own sportbike-building firm with the Motor Company's blessing. In 1993, Harley took a stronger interest in Buell's project, and together they formed a new Buell company. Buell's S1 Lightning was powered by a highly tuned 1,203-cc Harley V-twin, and won rave reviews from a new breed of Harley fans. (Photograph © Andrew Morland)*

"The concept of the 'motorcycle outlaw' was as uniquely American as jazz."
—Hunter S. Thompson,
Hell's Angels: A Strange and Terrible Saga, 1966

1977 Harley-Davidson XLCR

In the days when café racers were the hot ticket and trick Ducati V-twins and Dunstall Nortons ruled the roads, Harley-Davidson designer Willie G. Davidson crafted a café racer of his own. Based on the Sportster, the XLCR blended styling lines from café racers, road racers, and dirt trackers, and wrapped the whole package in black with chromed highlights. But the XLCR was too much too soon, and never sold well when new. Today, however, the world's a different place, and the XLCR is a hot collectible commodity. Owner: Jerri Grindle. (Photograph © Andrew Morland)

Chapter 2

Making History

"Don't you know you can get the same sensations by tying firecrackers to your legs and sitting over an oil heater?"
—Collier's *magazine, 1913*

With all of the intensity of archaeologists digging up dirt on the past, the history of the Harley-Davidson Motor Company has been excavated, analyzed, and argued over by academics, lawyers, historians, and regular folk alike.

Now, the historians tell their own stories of what inspired them and how they wrote their versions of Harley-Davidson history.

1915 Harley-Davidson Model 11F
Harley-Davidson's laurels have long rested on its famous V-twins, but it was not until 1909—a long six years after the Motor Company was founded— that the firm released its first V-twin-engined motorcycle. To add to the irony, that 1909 V-twin did not return for the 1910 model year. It was not until 1911 that the V-twin was back to stay. The 11-hp, 45-degree, V-twin displaced the now-classic 61 cubic inches (1,000 cc). Owner: Shaun Baker. (Photograph © Andrew Morland)

My First Motorcycle . . . and What It Led To

By Harry V. Sucher

Harry V. Sucher has been a pioneer in recording motorcycle history. His famous histories of Indian and Harley-Davidson are the first books many enthusiasts found when looking for information on their favorite cycles. His books include *The Iron Redskin: A History of the Indian Motorcycle*, *Harley-Davidson: The Milwaukee Marvel*, and most recently *Inside American Motorcycling And The American Motorcycle Association 1900 to 1999*.

Harry began riding in the 1920s. He had the rare opportunity to examine classic models when they were brand new and to become friends with many of motorcycling's greats—riders, racers, dealers, and engineers.

In this essay, he talks about the thrills that surrounded motorcycling in its infant days when the present was a brave new world.

In addition to my early memory of attending the first Armistice Day celebration in 1918 when I was three years old, I recall that the next year saw the arrival of my second cousin, Joel Martin, on a 1914 single-geared Harley-Davidson at my home in Santa Rosa, California. Joel had taken twenty-eight days to travel from Indianapolis aboard that cycle, and he told of experiencing numerous punctures along the way, as well as getting mired in mud and encountering heavy weather.

In the excitement of the day, I was just able to spell out the words "Harley-Davidson" on the tanks and marvel at the huge Solar headlight on the front of the machine. Joel, meanwhile, spent twenty-four hours sleeping off the effects of the adventure.

About this time, I was treated to several rides on the rear saddle of a 1918 Powerplus Indian by one Joseph Tisserand. By now, I was thoroughly captivated by motorcycling.

My preoccupation with motorsport in the post–World War I era was heightened by the building of the Cotati Speedway at Cotati, California, a village about seven miles south of Santa Rosa. This vast edifice, a mile and a half in circumference, was made of wood and was built under the supervision of Jack Prince, who had built several large tracks in 1914 in different parts of the country. I recall visiting the site of this board track during its construction with Prince

Harley-Davidson memories
The past was the best of times and the worst of times: Everyone reminisces about it, but few would want to live it again. This collection of Harley memorabilia dates from the 1930s, which were tough, yet rewarding years for the Motor Company. With motorcycle sales down during the Great Depression, Harley had to fight tooth and nail with rival Indian for wins on the racetracks and sales on the showroom floors. In 1935, Harley-Davidson finally unveiled its secret weapon, the overhead-valve Series E Knucklehead that would become the company's savior. Memorabilia owners: Ron Sabie and Russ Sierck. (Photograph © Nick Cedar)

himself seen driving an elegant red buggy pulled by a well-groomed sorrel horse. The track was built of several carloads of lumber specially ordered from nearby Duncans Mills. In addition, carloads of iron spikes were on hand to hold the structure together.

There was much fanfare in Santa Rosa with the opening of the track in 1921 and to heighten interest in car races, a number of racing cars were towed through the main street of town with their engines running.

Initial races featured such immortals as Jimmy Murphy, Tommy Milton, Ralph de Palma, and Peter de Paoli in the car racing class as well as motorcycling entrants such as Ralph Hepburn, Shrimp Barns, and Ray Seymour. The latter did a 117-mph solo circuit as an exhibition lap. The grand opening of the track featured the Santa Rosa marching band with flags and bunting adding to the color of the scene.

The 1922 racing season again featured well-known stars of the board track and I attended no fewer than three of the auto and motorcycle races in the company of my father.

The 1923 races saw the end of the track as builder Jack Prince suffered a paralytic stroke and interest in this type of event waned due to the large number of fatal accidents.

The track itself was located in an area known as Denmans Flats and was worthless for agriculture due to the adobe content of the soil. Through lack of use and its rapid deterioration from wind and weather, the edifice was dismantled in 1925.

I became deeply interested in motorcycling history as I matured and began collecting catalogs and sales manuals covering the industry and the sport. Angelo Rossi opened his Indian dealership in Santa Rosa in 1921 and Joe Frugoli opened his Harley operation in 1925. Each of these small dealerships was operated single-handedly with Rossi handling bicycle sales to augment his modest income.

My own entrance into motorcycle ownership was through Frank Fontaine, a friend in Santa Rosa slightly older than myself. We entered into partnership in the purchase of a Harley-Davidson M Type motorcycle with a 37-ci opposed Sport Twin engine as manufactured from 1919 to 1922. No lighting was required as the machine had a magneto and was not fitted with headlights. The machine was basically sound although it showed signs of use. The purchase price was $10. We each put up a five-dollar bill.

In those days, the roads were mostly gravel and only the state highways were paved. This meant that surfaces on the secondary roads were in various states of repair as they were largely gravel, full of washboarding. A friendly deputy sheriff informed us that we didn't need a license if we stayed off the main roads. While the speed of this middleweight bike was modest, the road surfaces were such that high speed was precluded in any case. Fontaine's older brother cleaned the carburetor and fixed a new set of ignition points, so under moderate use the machine never broke down.

In due time Fontaine decided that he was going to buy a car and we agreed that his half of the bike was now worth $7.50, which I happily paid. The machine was now all mine and I enjoyed another year of modest travel on Sonoma County's backroads. I was fifteen at the time.

I subsequently purchased a 1925 Model T Ford roadster for use in inclement weather. This cost me $12.50 as I had to replace the back tires, which were worn through to the fabric.

In 1931, I purchased a well-worn J Model V-twin Harley, which gave way to a 1927 Indian Chief. I liked the riding position on the Chief better because it was one of the champion skidders of all time with its clincher-style tires.

1940s Harley-Davidson WR

Facing page: *Armando Magri was a well-known national-level Harley racer in the 1930s and 1940s who won many a race aboard his Harley-Davidson WR. The model was launched in 1941 to combat Indian's reigning Sport Scout, and it soon became a favorite of privateer racers everywhere in "showroom stock" Class C events. The WR's iron-barreled, side-valve, 45-ci (750-cc) V-twin engine was almost bulletproof, and the three-speed gearbox was all that was needed for dirt-tracking. Amazingly, the WR still won races for years after it went out of production. Armando, meanwhile, went on to own and operate the Sacramento, California, Harley-Davidson dealership for many years. (Photograph © Nick Cedar)*

"King of the Road"

Overleaf: *An old-timer recounts a tale of Harley history in this oil painting of a Harley dealership by artist Dave Barnhouse. (the Hadley Companies)*

NEIDENGARD'S
CYCLE CENTER
AIR HERE
Drink
ROYAL CROWN
COLA
Best By taste-test
RC
Katie
Loves
Johnny
Adam

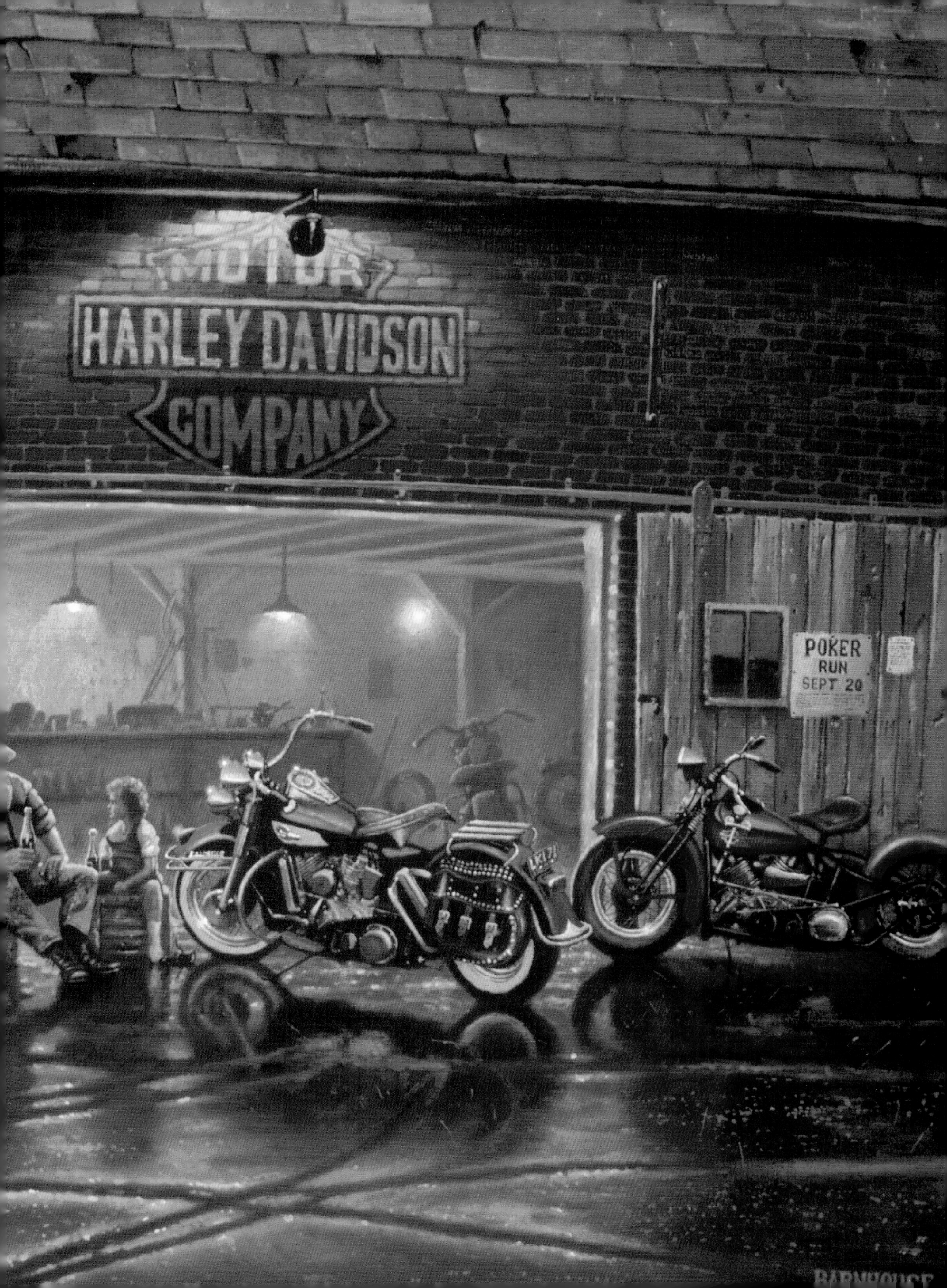
MOTOR
HARLEY DAVIDSON
COMPANY
POKER
RUN
SEPT 20

1921 Harley-Davidson Model W Sport Twin
In 1918, the Motor Company was fearing for its future. Automobile sales were soaring but motorcycle sales were plummeting. Harley had its V-twins and singles, but decided that an inexpensive, lightweight cycle would turn sales around. In 1919, the utilitarian Model W Sport was introduced, powered by a 35.6-ci (584-cc) flat twin. While it was a solid, well-engineered machine, the Sport never caught on with cyclists—and didn't make many converts. Harley pulled the plug on its production in 1923. Owner: Armando Magri. (Photograph © Nick Cedar)

In the meantime, my interest in motorcycle history was very much alive and through my grandmother I received a modest, unexpected subsidy for pursuing the subject.

In 1932, I made the acquaintance of Nelson Bettencourt when I visited Benicia, California, where he was located. I was visiting my cousin, Lt. J. G. Sucher of Benicia Arsenal. Bettencourt introduced me to other motorcycle people and at that time I expanded my relationship with many other dealers.

My investigation into further motorcycle history occurred between 1932 and 1940 when I made the acquaintance of and interviewed Vernon Guthrie, Thomas Callahan Butler, and almost everybody who was anybody in the motorcycling field. The culmination of my research into motorcycling resulted in the publication of three definitive histories: *The Iron Redskin: A History of the Indian Motorcycle* in 1977, *Harley-Davidson: The Milwaukee Marvel* in 1981, and my latest effort, *Inside American Motorcycling And The American Motorcycle Association 1900 to 1999*. I have also contributed numerous articles to motorcycling publications through the years and continue to do so whenever I feel I have something to offer to the motorcycling public.

Harley racer, 1920s

From the days when it took iron men to ride the iron machines, this Harley jockey sits astraddle his single-cylinder racer with his newly won trophy resting on the tank. (Library of Congress)

Catching Up On History

By David K. Wright

These days, bookstore and cycle-shop shelves are chock full of tomes about Harley-Davidson. That wasn't the case in 1980, however, when David K. Wright was asked to research and write a history of the Motor Company. What he learned literally filled a book—*The Harley-Davidson Motor Company: An Official History*, which went on to sell some 85,000 hardcover copies in three editions.

As a freelance writer, David is also the author of numerous other books on a variety of subjects, but his history of the Motor Company holds a special place in his heart.

Here are his thoughts about the company, the cycles, and about Harley-Davidson personnel, past and present.

As the 100th anniversary of Harley-Davidson approaches, I have the motorcycle manufacturer in a Catch-22 situation. A Catch-22, as you know, is a problem in which the only solution is denied by an inherent rule. In the case of Harley-Davidson and myself, I signed a contract in 1980 to write a company history. The contract stated that Harley-Davidson personnel would exercise "editorial oversight"—censorship. However, the contract continued, if the book were to go out of print, all rights would revert to the author. And because Harley-Davidson decided in 1996 to stop selling the book through its dealers, *The Harley-Davidson Motor Company* went out of print and I retain all rights.

Now that I have them in this Catch-22, I'm not sure what to do with them. Looking back, I'm surprised at how unimportant the contract turned out to be. After all, during 1980–1982, the executives were so busy trying to save the company that they paid little attention to my writing. I was able to reveal approximately 90 percent of the dirt anyone else ever heard, saw, or dug up. Here is the other 10 percent, which may not be gossip exactly, but which needs to appear in print somewhere, sometime. . . .

The following anecdote is about Vaughn Beals, the man who led Harley-Davidson from the brink of ruin to giddy prosperity. The venue was MECCA, a cavernous Milwaukee hall where, in August 1982, dealers were being introduced to 1983 models. I thought the best-looking bike on the floor was the new Roadster. The only problem with the show bike was a chrome piece on the instrument panel that fell off at the slightest touch. Beals matter-of-factly told Harley-Davidson engineers to either fix it or remove the prototype bike from the floor. See, he

Catching up with speeders, 1950s

Harley-Davidson–mounted traffic cop Jayne Mansfield pulls over yet another speeder and issues a ticket in this far-fetched promotional photograph. (Library of Congress)

knew that dealers had put up with that kind of annoying inattention to quality, and he'd had enough of it. The bezel or whatever was repaired and the bike was well received. But I view this incident as the point at which Harley-Davidson began to walk the quality walk.

Dealers had good memories. They knew that each uncrated Harley required tweaking in order to get it ready for the customer. Six months before Vaughn Beals's fix-it-or-move-it dictum, I was sitting in a tent at Daytona with a long-time Midwestern Harley-Davidson dealer. Noticing that I'd put away notebook and tape recorder, he leaned toward me and said, "I sell Harleys and I sell Suzukis. Last year, I sold 125 Harley-Davidsons and 250 Suzukis. I have four full-time Harley mechanics and one Suzuki mechanic. What does that tell you about quality?" That was the moment I realized everyone connected with the motorcycle knew quality had to improve.

Wake-up calls were widespread in 1982. I happened to be at the Harley-Davidson offices on Juneau Avenue when the cycle mags showing the 1983 models were delivered. From the guy making copies to the fellows in the boardroom, all were stunned at the Harley-Davidson look-alike bikes being created, apparently without warning, in Japan. Honda, Kawasaki, Suzuki, Yamaha—all of them suddenly were selling cruisers powered by V-twins. Adding insult to injury, Japanese bikes at the time were simply faster and more reliable than the Milwaukee offering. It was not a fun day at the factory.

Compounding problems, Harley-Davidson's core buyers were complaining about everything. Jeff Bleustein, engineering vice president at the time, was criticized for hiring engineers who didn't necessarily know anything about motorcycles. The company was blasted for having Japanese suppliers, despite the fact that there frequently were no domestic makers of bike

carburetors, for example. At about this time, Goodyear stopped making cycle tires; what was an All-American guy to do when his dresser or Sportster needed new shoes? There were even some complaints from South Dakotans in the wake of the factory naming a bike after that utterly Harley annual affair in the town of Sturgis. The company seemed damned if it did and damned if it didn't.

Harley-Davidson had a run of bad luck. In 1981, the company commissioned Porsche to design a prototype bike. Somehow, the one-of-a-kind machine's existence was leaked to the press. Core buyers went crazy, in part because the design was offshore and in part because they only wanted V-twin power. Meanwhile, execution of the Evolution V-2 engine was not going well. The foundry supplying heads was experiencing pinhole problems that seemed to take forever to iron out. Commendably, Harley-Davidson made sure the new motor was right before installing it in their machines beginning in 1986.

So how did Harley-Davidson become the best-selling cycle in America in 1999? This part is no secret: the company rounded up a pile of dough by selling shares of stock beginning in 1986. The money realized bought Harley-Davidson time to greatly improve the way the products were made and worked, it gave the company saddlebags full of favorable publicity, and it allowed Harley marketers to perfect the parts and accessories business and H.O.G., the dealer-centered Harley-Davidson club that has helped put the average retailer of Harley-Davidsons on easy street.

The company has come a long way since my book first came out. Virtually broke in the early 1980s, the guys in charge seemed best at going off on extended bike tours every time a crisis arose.

How times change.

"Potato-potato-potato."
—The sound of an idling Harley-Davidson V-twin,
according to Harley's trademark attorney Joseph Bonk,
who was involved in filing the sound with the
U.S. Patent and Trademark Office in 1994

Making history
*Proud workers construct the latest and
greatest on the Motor Company's
York, Pennsylvania, assembly lines.
(Photographs © Jerry Irwin)*

Black Leathers and a Stiff Upper Lip

By Roy Bacon

Roy Bacon is a walking encyclopedia of motorcycling. Mention a make or model, and he can recite its specifications, variations, and historical tribulations. Ask about a certain race, and he knows who won at what speed and on what machine.

It should thus come as little surprise that Roy is also one of the world's most prolific authors of books on motorcycling and automobiles. From his home on the Isle of Wight, Roy has written histories of motorcycle makes from Triumph to Honda, BMW to BSA.

In this essay, he evokes the years when Harley-Davidson first came to Great Britain and evolved from being an unobtainable symbol of America to becoming part of popular culture.

 Just after World War II, there were a good number of Harleys to be found in the United Kingdom, but nearly all were ex-War Department machines in a variety of conditions. There were few prewar machines. The large number of ex-WD motorcycles—a British version of the American term "war surplus"—came about as the services found that they had far too many machines for their postwar, peacetime needs and proposed to sell off the surplus at auctions up and down the country.

Riders had the happy idea that they would be able to visit the auction area, pick out an individual machine, bid for it, and carry it home—maybe even ride it if they had picked well. In fact, petrol was severely rationed at that time—at one stage only available to essential users—so there was little chance of finding enough fuel to run to the other side of

town, much less on to the next town. It also became clear that the machines would be sold in lots to dealers and this duly happened.

All the machines were still in their khaki of various shades depending on the army that had used them, and dealers reckoned that this color would lack appeal to the British buyers after six years of war. The solution was simple: Fill the paint gun with black paint, stand the machine against a convenient wall, and spray it, tires and all. Turn it around and repeat for the other side.

Such machines would remain khaki where the paint missed, under the fenders or tank, and most seemed to survive with black-painted high-tension leads, fuel pipes, and cables.

One or two enterprising dealers chose to use maroon, maybe in the hope of standing out from the crowd, more likely because they had stumbled across a bargain in that color from another ex-WD sale. In those days, maroon was not a good color for motor-

1943 Harley-Davidson WLC

The Motor Company's WLC and WLA mil-spec models were built in the tens of thousands for the Allied forces during World War II. Following the war, the surviving machines were honorably discharged into civilian hands and often served faithfully for years after in civvies. This WLC was restored in Canadian Royal Air Force colors. Owner: Mark Bently. (Photograph © Andrew Morland)

cycles or cars for it would always fade after a few years. However, makers who persisted with it for each new generation would fall for the shade in the showroom and find out the hard way. Only much later did technology improve and come up with a fade-proof maroon.

Back in the early postwar years no one cared too much as new machines were hard to find. The politicians had their cry of "Export or Die," us not them of course, and most production went overseas leaving the home market struggling to keep prewar machines running. One helpful aspect was that most used an Amal carburetor and Lucas electrics and there were plenty of ex-WD spares about that would fill a gap. In the very early postwar days, anyone lucky enough to purchase a new machine had to sign a covenant to retain it for at least two years and not sell it as this would have been an easy way to make a good profit, such was the demand.

Life was no easier for the makers whose allocation of material was based on prewar production figures. This was fine for people such as BSA and Triumph but not for Phil Vincent. Hence the large amount of aluminum in his machine, plenty of this being available in aircraft factories, and the minimum number of steel tubes.

The postwar Harleys were nearly all ex-WD, WLA, or WLC 45s handled by a small number of dealers who sold them at a competitive price. The smaller Indians were also to be found but both marques had little spare-part support from the United States. However, machines too far gone to sell could be broken for parts, and more came from the ex-WD parts stocks that were also sold off by the services.

At that time there was no question of importing new machines from the United States, the trade just had to go the other way to help the balance of payments problems of Britain. The export drive was assisted by the number of U.S. servicemen who had sampled British machines while in Europe and bought them once back home again. Now, many of those BSAs, Nortons, and Triumphs are being re-imported back to the United Kingdom for the classic market. Then, the import of Harley-Davidson models into the United Kingdom was prohibited for many years by currency controls that applied to many products of that era.

Later—much later and well into the 1950s—it did become possible to import machines from the United States into Britain, but by that time Indian had gone with its United Kingdom reputation somewhat blemished by the Corgi and later Brave models involved with the Brockhouse firm. The real problem remained the import duty charged to bring the machines over for this pushed up retail prices to a level very few would be prepared to pay.

By late 1957, the Duo-Glide models were £689 or £723 while the Sportster was £639. This at a time when the popular twins from BSA, Norton, and Triumph were all under £300. At the other end of the scale, the 165-cc two-stroke Hummer was listed at £268 when the 148-cc BSA Bantam was £113. It was hardly surprising that demand was small for the Big Twins and non-existent for the two-stroke.

At that time British riders saw the Harleys as large, ponderous V-twins with too much equipment, poor performance for their engine size, and limited handling and brakes. Few riders had any experience with the marque and that was mostly with the ex-WD models, hardly the most inspiring, especially after they had served their time in the army.

Few people visited the United States in those days, prior to mass air travel, so little was known of the long, straight interstate highways that were best traveled with a big, soft engine that could carry rider and pillion all day long in ease and comfort. In Brit-

1929 Harley-Davidson D

Facing page, top: *Harley-Davidson's new D Series arrived in 1929 powered by a 45-ci (750-cc) side-valve V-twin. Designed to do battle with Indian's famed Series 101 Scout, the Forty-Five upped the ante by using a constant-mesh transmission. Owner: Eldon Brown. (Photograph © John Dean/Reynolds-Alberta Museum)*

1916 Harley-Davidson racer

Facing page, bottom: *"Shorty" Tompkins boasted a long racing resumé from the 1930s through the 1950s. He dominated AMA District 36 racing, and once held a world record for the quarter-mile dirt track. He finally quit racing in 1951, having sustained various injuries over the years. Shorty continued to restore and refurbish a variety of antique motorcycles, such as this unrestored inlet-over-exhuast-valve Harley V-twin racer. The cycle was set up for board-track racing, although it featured a rear band brake, which was probably added later. (Photograph © Nick Cedar)*

1942 Harley-Davidson WLA

Above: *Patriotism was the inspiration for Harley-Davidson's mil-spec WLC and WLA models. When the U.S. Army sought to draft motorcycles to do battle in World War II, the Motor Company recast its civilian WL in olive drab and furnished it with special military appointments. This fully equipped U.S. Army WLA was powered by a side-valve, 45-degree, V-twin of 45 cubic inches (750 cc). Most importantly, the WLA proved reliable with minimal maintenance. This is one of almost 90,000 produced. Owner: Ian Cottrell Broadwey. (Photograph © Andrew Morland)*

ain, the roads twisted and turned and ran through towns; this called for light and nimble machines with good brakes, handling, and acceleration. Fuel was expensive and heavily taxed, so consumption was far more important while tax and insurance costs favored small motorcycles.

The charm of the big Harley was unknown and hard to appreciate in Britain, although the long, straight roads of France and Germany did allow the marque to stretch its legs. In time, Britain added motorways and more people visited the United States so the benefits of the Harley style became much better known.

Image changed as well. Reports in the motorcycle press of U.S. events highlighted Daytona and one or two of the major off-road events such as the Jack Pine and Big Bear. We all heard that Elvis rode a motorcycle but fewer realized that it was a KH Harley and while the young flocked to buy his records and see his films, older people often criticized what they failed to understand about his music. Black leathers tended to be associated with the irresponsible, the loud and awkward troublemakers, and change that was not always welcome.

Few, even keen, motorcyclists really appreciated how good the Harley was at its job in the United States, or just how fast and well developed that 45-degree V-twin engine was. Nothing was known of how far back this went, of running on board tracks at 80 mph plus in 1911, or at well over 100 mph in the early 1920s, or of the performances on the half- and one-mile tracks.

Many years later the Brits traveled much more

"Rocky's Garage"

James "Kingneon" Guçwa's oil-on-canvas painting portrays a classic American gas station on the side of a classic blue highway. (Painting © 1999/Courtesy of Leslie Levy Creative Art Licensing)

to the United States, and found that a big V-twin was just the job for the roads out there and more suited to their own back home now that they were straighter and longer. Hence the surge of interest in recent times with the big Harley becoming a common sight in the United Kingdom. It may have taken time, but the Harley-Davidson stand now rivals any other at the annual Motorcycle Show held in the Midlands each year.

1983 Harley-Davidson XR1000

It's undoubtedly fate that some of the models considered in retrospect to be among Harley-Davidson's best were machines that didn't sell when new. The XLCR café racer proved the point, as did the XR1000. Created as an XR750 racer for the street, the XR1000 was a thoroughbred hot rod. Its tuned 998-cc engine boasted trick cylinder heads and dual Dell'Orto carburetors sourced from the XR. In standard tune, it put out 70 hp at 6,000 rpm, rocketing the 470-pound (213-kg) sled to a top speed of 120 mph (193 kph). Owner: Jim Wild. (Photograph © John Dean/Reynolds-Alberta Museum)

History According to Harley-Davidson

1901: Twenty-one-year-old William S. Harley and his childhood pal, twenty-year-old Arthur Davidson, start designing a single-cylinder gas-fueled engine following the style set by France's Count de Dion and Georges Bouton.

1903: Two or three—the numbers are disputed—Harley-Davidson "motor bicycles" are built, followed by two or three more in 1904. By 1905, production had more than doubled to seven cycles. The first Harley was sold before it was finished to a local man named Meyer, who put 6,000 miles (9,645 km) on the machine before selling it to George Lyon, who added 15,000 miles (24,135 km). It then went through three more owners and traveled 62,000 additional miles (99,758 km). Harley-Davidson proudly advertised in 1913 that the first machine had more than 100,000 miles (160,900 km) under its belt.

1907: The Harley-Davidson Motor Company is incorporated. The new firm builds and sells one sole product: the 4-hp Silent Gray Fellow.

1909: Bill Harley unveils his first 45-degree 61-ci (1,000-cc) V-twin, made by grafting a second cylinder onto his existing single.

1910: Harley-Davidson now employs 149 workers.

1914: Bill Harley establishes the firm's first official racing department.

1916: Harley-Davidsons are drafted by the U.S. Army and mounted with machine guns on their sidecars. A new motorized cavalry under the command of General "Black Jack" Pershing sets off to chase Pancho Villa in northern Mexico.

1917: Harley-Davidson introduces a full line of bicycles.

1917–1918: During World War I, the Allies are armed with more than 20,000 Harley-Davidsons.

1918: Harley-Davidson boasts more than 2,000 dealers around the world, from Tasmania to Europe, Japan to Iceland.

1920: Harley-Davidson is the largest motorcycle maker in the world in both factory floor space and number of machines produced. *The Enthusiast* magazine debuts.

1929: WL 45-ci side-valve model is unveiled.

1931: Three-wheeled Servi-Car is introduced.

1935: The Model 61 OHV "Knucklehead" is first shown to dealers—although it will be months before the cycle is widely available.

1941–1946: During World War II, Harley-Davidson builds 88,000 military cycles, most of them the 45-ci WLA and WLC models.

1947: Media hype surrounding a fracas on the Fourth of July at Hollister, California, inspires public fear of a new type of outlaw, the biker.

1948: A revised and refined version of the 61- and 74-ci Knucklehead arrives with the moniker "Panhead."

1953: Harley-Davidson celebrates its fiftieth anniversary. *The Wild One* debuts with Marlon Brando on a Triumph Thunderbird and Lee Marvin as the "bad" outlaw biker on a Harley-Davidson.

1957: The Sportster, powered by a 55-ci overhead-valve V-twin, debuts.

1961: Harley-Davidson becomes majority owner of Aermacchi motorcycles of Italy and begins importing the lightweight machines into the United States.

1962: Harley-Davidson unveils its new golf cart line.

1964: The Hell's Angels are catapulted into the national spotlight following a wild beach-party brouhaha over Labor Day weekend near Big Sur, California.

1965: Dawn of the "Shovelhead" engine. Harley-Davidson first offers an "electric leg"—and electric starter—on the Electra-Glide.

1966: Brigitte Bardot has a hit with the Serge Gainsbourg–penned song "Harley-Davidson," featuring the statement "I don't need anyone else on my Harley-Davidson."

1968: Harley-Davidson produces only 15,475 motorcycles. The failing company is sold to sporting goods conglomerate AMF.

1969: *Easy Rider* opens with Peter Fonda as Captain America and Dennis Hopper as Billy setting off across America on their Harley choppers.

1970: A motorcycle daredevil by the name of Evel Knievel joins forces with Harley-Davidson and begins performing stunts on an XR-750.

1971: Designer Willie G. Davidson's first factory custom, the FX Super Glide, debuts with a patriotic red-white-and-blue paint scheme.

1973: Motorcycle assembly is moved from the venerable Milwaukee factory to a new facility in York, Pennsylvania.

1974: Evel Knievel attempts to jump Idaho's Snake River Canyon with his jet-powered "SkyCycle." Robert M. Pirsig's *Zen and the Art of Motorcycle Maintenance* is published.

1981: A group of Harley-Davidson executives led by Vaughn Beals acquires the firm from AMF.

1984: The new aluminum Evolution V^2 engine, sometimes known as the "Blockhead," is launched.

1994: Harley-Davidson files with the U.S. Patent and Trademark Office to register the *sound* of its V-twin engine as a trademark. Harley's trademark attorney, Joseph Bonk, compares the sound to a spud, stating that the idle sounds like "*potato–potato–potato.*"

1998: Harley-Davidson buys majority ownership in ex-Harley designer Erik Buell's sportbike-building firm and plans a full line of innovative Harley-powered café racers.

1999: Harley-Davidson engineers introduce the Twin Cam 88.

2000: Harley-Davidson engineers introduce the Twin Cam 88B, the first counterbalanced V-twin engine in the company's history, for use in the Softail line.

• Buell introduces the single-cylinder Blast entry-level motorcycle.

• Harley-Davidson engineers introduce fuel injection technology for use in the Softail line.

2001: Harley-Davidson engineers introduce the V-Rod, which features the first liquid-cooled V-twin engine used in a Harley-Davidson street bike.

2002: Buell introduces the aluminum-framed Firebolt.

2003: Former racing director Dick O'Brien, arguably the most successful racing director in Harley-Davidson's history (with 16 Grand National Championships and 183 individual championships between 1960 and 1983), passes away.

2004: Harley-Davidson announces that it is building a museum.

• Andrew Hines clinches his first NHRA Powerade Pro Stock Motorcycle Championship aboard a Screamin' Eagle/Vance & Hines Harley-Davidson motorcycle.

• Harley-Davidson engineers introduce rubber-mounted engines to the Sportster line.

2005: Andrew Hines wins his second straight NHRA Powerade Pro Stock Motorcycle Championship.

2006: Harley-Davidson engineers introduce six-speed transmissions to the Dyna line.

• Harley-Davidson opens its first dealership in mainland China.

2008: Harley-Davidson purchases MV Agusta Group, which builds MV Agusta and Cagiva motorcycles in Italy, from Claudio Castiglioni for $109 million.

• Harley-Davidson engineers introduce a new touring-bike frame.

• The Harley-Davidson Museum opens its doors to the public.

2009: Harley-Davidson announces its first three-wheeler since the demise of the Servi-Car.

• Harley-Davidson expands into the Indian market.

2010: Harley-Davidson sells MV Agusta Group back to Claudio Castiglioni for less than $5 million.

2011: Eddie Krawiec wins Harley-Davidson's fifth drag-racing title.

2014: Harley-Davidson engineers introduce partial liquid cooling for the top end of some touring models.

Chapter 3

On the Road

*"I don't want a pickle,
I just want to ride my motor-sickle."*
—Arlo Guthrie, *The Motorcycle Song*

The alchemy that a Harley-Davidson motorcycle and the open road produce was summed up perfectly in the 1970s by the Motor Company itself. The ad slogan read, "The Great American Freedom Machine," and rarely has an advertising copywriter gotten it so right.

The image of The Great American Freedom Machine was perfect for the 1970s, but it is also ideal for defining what a Harley-Davidson means for riders of almost any time and any place. Whether you are flexing your motorcycle's muscles on a neverending highway or simply dashing down to the store to buy milk, Harley-Davidson motorcycles are built for the road.

On the road
Chasing the horizon en route to a small town called Sturgis, South Dakota. (Photograph © Jerry Irwin)

The Speedster

THE roads are dry, the sky is clear,
There is no sign of dust;
My bus I now will have to mount,
Or else I'll surely bust.

I take it out and tune it up,
Then mount it for a spin;
And gradually I speed it up
Until I get pulled in.

Lo! now I stand before the judge,
And tell my tale of woe;
When he announces ten and costs,
I hand him all my dough.

My spirits quickly droop and fade;
I start my boat in gloom,
As all along the road ahead,
The coppers seem to loom.

But in a week it's all forgot,
As is the way with men,
And I begin to hit it up,
Until I'm pinched again.

And so it goes from month to month,
When riding in a hurry,
And we get pinched from time to time;
But then, "Oh, we should worry!"

Hix

In Pursuit of the Unholy Grail

By Cook Neilson

Cook Neilson is a legend. He was the editor of *Cycle* magazine from 1970 to 1979, and is today a sometimes studio photographer.

But Cook's renown rests on the motorcycles he built. Every racer knows the tale of the "California Hot-Rod," the mythical Ducati 750 SS built by Cook and ridden by Phil Schilling to beat the factory guys at their own game.

Cook began his cycling career with a Harley-Davidson 883 Sportster, which to this day wears a halo in his memory.

At the end of June 1963, my otherwise utterly empty head contained but three ideas: 1) That I had to have a motorcycle; 2) that "Meeting the Nicest People" was a non-starter; and 3) that time was running out.

I had just completed my freshman year in college and, as I saw it, my future was inevitable. Finish with school, sign up for some kind of military service, then strap on a necktie and forage earnestly through a predictable world. If I was going to wedge a bike into my life somewhere it had to be . . . now.

Motorcycling's tilting landscape thirty-five years ago, at least as far as streetbikes were concerned, held more variations than you can imagine. But the strictures of time concentrated my focus toward the higher altitudes, and enthroned there was the first of my two favorite motorcycles: The Harley-Davidson XLCH Sportster, 1964 version, 883 cc, $1,435, V-twin, perfect primary imbalance. As soon as I saw it

at Tommy Hannum's dealership in Media, Pennsylvania, I knew that this was a telegram edged in black, and that it was mine.

By the time I finally parted company with my Harley ten years later (only a cut-down primary cover and a heavily modified Fairbanks-Morse magneto were left from the original) we had gotten ourselves thrown out of college for a year; removed from Pennsylvania's list of citizens with valid operator's licenses (122 in a 50); dragooned into the military; reduced in rank from sergeant to one pay grade below private for an incident involving nitromethane, tire smoke, and a commander with a diminished sense of humor; and into four good-sized wrecks, only three of which were our fault.

Along the way, my CH served as a commuter vehicle, a means of visiting my girlfriend, a long-distance touring bike, a three-time Bonneville record-holder and, briefly, an NHRA Top Fuel record holder. Early on, it carried me around the legendary Grafton Scrambles track one lovely summer's day. I used it to sell encyclopedias door-to-door in Louisville, Ken-

"The Speedster"

This quaint poem graced the pages of a motorcycling magazine in 1913.

tucky, and to get to my job in a cement factory in Tampa, Florida. Later, before I sold it, my Sportster logged a quarter-mile trap speed of over 170 mph at Orange County International Raceway's dragstrip.

For ten years the bike was more than a noisy adjunct—it was a defining presence in my life, and it reshuffled everything. After Bonneville in 1966, I wrote a little piece for Harley-Davidson's magazine *The Enthusiast*, and just before I graduated from college in 1967, I sent a story to *Cycle World* about Sonny Routt's double-engined Triumph dragster that editor Ivan Wagar actually published. By September of that year, I was on the staff of *Cycle* magazine in New York City, and my life had swung onto an arc that I couldn't have imagined four years earlier.

Not to say that the Sportster was a particularly brilliant motorcycle. On some cold days it would take as long as an hour to start. For as long as I used it as a streetbike it made its way down the road with a quaint, weaving motion that applications of steering damper merely aggravated, and it could never get very far down that road because the fuel tank only held 2¼ gallons. It vibrated with a determination unmatched by any motorcycle that I ever rode, and when we goosed displacement from 883 cc up to 1,000 cc for Bonneville in 1966, the jackhammering got

even worse. The suspension wasn't so hot either, and neither were the brakes. It burned out alternators and fried voltage regulators and defilimented headlamps.

But this is irrelevant sniveling, because the XLCH was never about "good," it was about horsepower, and through the years my pursuit of this unholy grail led me to people like Jerry Branch, Tom Sifton, Dick O'Brien, and George Smith, and to chemicals like nitromethane, benzene, methanol, and the nastiest of all, propylene oxide. The chase for more and more power also caused me to become intimately familiar with engine internals, since nitro has a way of making internals . . . external. (A conversation I'll never forget: My friend Charlie Kowchak came with me

to Bonneville in 1969. We were running what was called a "heavy load"—95 percent nitro, 5 percent propylene oxide. Charlie, driving the tow car, met me at the end of the track after a memorable qualifying attempt.

"How'd it go?" he asked.

"Fine," I answered, "but I think I might have hurt it."

"Are you sure?" he asked.

"Just guessing," I said, "but there's a whole piston on top of the oil tank.")

As you may have figured by now, my Sportster never stayed the same for long. Like a little kid with a pile of Legos, I would change its pieces and put them together all different kinds of ways: stock streetbike; loud streetbike; loud modified streetbike;

1959 Harley-Davidson XLH Sportster

Left: *By the 1960s, Sportsters personified sporting cool. At the neon-lit drive-in restaurant on the edge of town, a Sportster won grudging looks of respect from British Triumph, Norton, and BSA owners, and many a main-street drag race ended with the Sportster leaving the vertical twins in the dust. This 1959 XLH wears its original Hi-Fi blue and Birch white color scheme. The overhead-valve, 54-cubic-inch (883-cc) engine was rated at 40 bhp at 5,500 rpm. Owner: Ida Newman of Loch Sheldrake, New York. (Photograph © Andrew Morland)*

Harley in drag

Below: *A Harley dragster lines up against a competitor to prove the breed. (Photograph © Jerry Irwin)*

loud modified streetbike/drag racer; Bonneville racebike; back to streetbike; all-out gasoline drag racer; all-out nitro-burning drag racer; nitro Bonneville bike; then, and finally, a nitro drag racer again.

Through it all, my CH was an indictable co-conspirator and unsavory influence, chuffing happily or exploding enthusiastically from Unionville, Pennsylvania, to Tampa, Florida, to New York City to Alton, Illinois, to Miami Beach to Wendover, Utah, to Los Angeles. We went everywhere and did everything, and at the end of the day, even though we had put a few dings and scratches on each other, my love for that bike was undiminished.

Favorite motorcycles aren't just about motorcycles; they're about experiences, good and bad, the more sharply drawn and luxuriantly colored the better. With my Sportster, I had plenty of both, certainly, but beyond that the bike deflected the trajectory of

my passage. Who knows? Without my Harley I might have become another goddamned lawyer.

One last thing: Back in 1963, while I was trying to figure out which was the Maximum Motorcycle, I remember the following in *Cycle World*'s road test of the 883 Sportster: "It'll grow hair on your chest, then part it down the middle." That road test sold me on the XLCH. It was written by *Cycle World*'s then-technical editor Gordon Jennings. By 1966, Gordon had been lured away to New York City by *Cycle*. Because I wanted to work for him, that's where I applied. Because I had a Sportster, he hired me.

Favorite motorcycles can't do any more for you than that.

Almost forgot. Earlier, I mentioned that the Sportster was one of my two favorite bikes. The other one is a certain 750-cc Ducati Desmo Super Sport, vintage circa 1974. V-Twin. It ended up with a displacement of exactly 883 cc. Go figure.

Waiting on a train
A passing vintage steam locomotive provides a pause on the road. (Photograph © Jerry Irwin)

Riding from the sunset
Above: *The sun may be sinking low, but the road runs on. (Photograph © Jerry Irwin)*

Flat-tracking
Right: *A blur of dizzying action, this Harley-Davidson XR-750–mounted rider moves up through the pack during a half-mile flat-track race. (Photograph © Jerry Irwin)*

A Work in Progress

By Timothy Remus

Timothy Remus is as handy with a camera and a pen as with a wrench. With a deep-rooted love for hot-rodded cars and customized motorcycles, he combined his talents and began writing magazine articles and books on his favorite subjects as well as preserving the cycles on film.

Timothy's books follow one of two styles: He has published coffee-table-style artbooks, including *The Customs of Arlen Ness* and *America's Best Harley-Davidson Customs*, and he has numerous how-to titles to his credit, such as his self-published *How to Build the Ultimate V-Twin Motorcycle* series.

This story of rebuilding and rebirth is one most motorcyclists can relate to, as many cycles always remain a work-in-progress.

 My ownership of Harleys runs parallel to my life as a photographer of Harleys and the men and women who build them. Unlike most of those bikes, however, my own machines tend to stay closer to stock.

The first was a Sportster. Money was tight at the time, as all my income came from freelance magazine and book work. (When you meet a freelancer in Sturgis or Daytona, buy that person a beer, because they probably don't have enough money in their pocket to buy one of their own.) The Sportster was only two years old when I bought it. The only obvious flaws were some paint blisters around the gas cap on the larger Sportster tank. With only 10,000 miles on the clock, I thought to myself, "Great, a no-maintenance motorcycle."

I should have known better.

The bike came from a dealership about forty miles from home. After getting the check from my banker, a friend gave me a ride over to the dealership, and I proudly took off on my "new" Sportster. A perfect summer day, I reveled in my own coolness as I rode the two-lane Wisconsin highways toward home just across the border in Minnesota. Life was good and getting better—until the bike bucked the first time and then quit altogether only five miles from my house.

With no tools other then a Swiss Army knife, I checked for gas, which flowed from the line like water from a fire hydrant. Next, I pulled one plug wire off to check for spark, hopefully without getting sparked myself or starting a fire. When I hit the button the blue spark jumped easily to the closest fin on the cylinder. Hmmmmm. So I put the plug wires back on, hit the button again, and the engine started right up.

That scenario happened again and again, even after I took it back to the dealership, until I finally

"Two Freespirits on a Motorcycle"
A motorcycle is always a work in progress. Witness these two bikers in this illustration from 1935.

replaced the errant circuit breaker that controlled the ignition. It would open on very hot days, only to close again by about the time I got around to checking for spark.

That winter I repainted the Sportster. I figured the blistered paint on the tank gave me all the excuse I needed. Actually, Mallard Teal in St. Paul did the paint, although he allowed me to do the grunt work of stripping and sanding the sheet metal and he even let me shoot some of the primer. When the next riding season rolled around, my little Sportster looked even better than it had before with its new two-tone candy paint job and a few new chrome trinkets.

By the second season, however, I'd discovered the Sportster's faults. Even with a small luggage rack bolted on the back, I could just barely get my camera gear strapped aboard. And riding double was best done for short distances.

When that next winter came around the Sportster went down the road and an old FXRT took over that same spot in the garage. Unlike the Sportster, the RT was definitely more than two years old, and the mileage on the odometer was nearly five times that on the Sportster. Looking it over, the phrase, "Run Hard and Put Up Wet" came to mind. But used Harleys weren't real plentiful that winter and the price was something I could afford. The best part was the Tour Pac, which was just the right size for my camera bag, and the backrest for my riding partner.

And every winter since it first came home, I've tried to improve the old girl. One year it's aesthetic considerations like a fresh paint job. The next year it might be a rebuild for the top end along with a better carburetor and the mandatory teardrop air cleaner.

When you meet me down the road, however, don't expect to find a perfectly restored and mildly customized FXRT. The lower legs are still nicked up and the paint on the frame leaves something to be desired. Like all Harleys, this one is a work in progress. Who knows, maybe by the time we meet I'll have the lower legs polished and the frame painted. Of course, the bike will still be in need of a new exhaust and I'd like to buy lowers for the fairing and wouldn't it be cool to squeeze a fatter rear tire into the stock swing arm?

"Berry Go Round"
A strawberry-themed fair ride provides a brilliant backdrop to the latest Harley in James "Kingneon" Guçwa's photorealistic oil painting on canvas. (Painting © 2000/ Courtesy of Leslie Levy Creative Art Licensing)

Riding Through Time:
A Knucklehead
Returns Home

By Buzz Kanter

Buzz Kanter got his first taste of motorcycles on a Honda QA50 while he was in ninth grade in the early 1970s. In college, he bought his first "real" motorcycle, a Honda 305 Superhawk. From there, he graduated to increasingly larger and faster motorcycles until he ended up on the motorcycle road-race circuit campaigning in various classes, including Superbike and Formula 2.

After retiring from the race circuit, Buzz's tastes shifted to classic motorcycles, primarily pre-1950 Harleys and Indians. Currently his favorite regular rides are his 1947 Harley Knucklehead and his 1946 Indian Chief.

Buzz Kanter is the founder and owner of TAM Communications, which publishes a number of magazines, including *American Iron Magazine* and *Motorcycle Tour & Cruiser*.

 Having ridden, rebuilt, and raced all sorts of motorcycles since the 1970s, I have experienced the romantic aspect of motorcycles, especially older ones. I'm not talking sex here, but the passion so many of us long-time riders experience with our motorcycles.

Part of my job as editor-in-chief at *American Iron Magazine* is to ride and review a lot of great new Harleys every year. Perhaps it's because I have such easy access to my choice of new machinery that I don't own a current-model Harley. I do own more than a dozen motorcycles and a favorite is my red 1947 Knucklehead that I've owned since 1994.

I first saw this machine at the Americade rally in Lake George, New York, in 1993. It sported a perfect cherry-red paint job, and my friend Tommy Richardson used it to draw in potential customers to sell them his Nortech-brand bike wash and detailing products.

I still remember clearly the first time that I saw him ride that sweet old handshifter down the main street in Lake George. The streets were swollen with the gleaming machinery that shows up for the Americade event, but I had eyes only for the Knucklehead. It was love at first sight. Even with the funky old fishtail exhaust Tommy had installed, this machine affected me deep down inside my soul. That night I made Tommy promise to call me if he ever considered selling this motorcycle.

If you've never had the good fortune of seeing a

Riding around the globe
This 1920s brochure illustration must have been wishful thinking from the Motor Company.

Knucklehead cruise by, you're missing an experience all Harley enthusiasts deserve. The first-year 1936 EL was the first "modern" Harley, and it is the machine all new Harley V-twins are based on. Sure you had to kickstart it to life and shifting the transmission was done by hand, but the engineers on Juneau Avenue got it right the first time with the Knucklehead. It was balanced in every sense of the word—visually, mechanically, and spiritually.

Introduced in 1935 at the annual Harley dealer's convention as a 1936 model, everyone there was blown away by this handsome new machine. The proportions were right on: The lines were both muscular and elegant with a hint of art deco. It was perfect for it's day and still a guaranteed head turner more than a half century later.

A year later I bumped into Tommy and his Knuck at the first day of the 1994 Sturgis rally and races. He was still riding it at night and using it as a display for his bike products during the day. I remember walking up and down in front of his display admiring every angle and detail of the bike. To me, it was a rolling piece of art and I wanted its image burned in my mind.

The next day, Tommy casually asked me if I was still interested in buying it. He mentioned there was another bike he wanted to buy in town and was short on cash. My heart missed a beat. Knowing how smart a horse trader Tommy was I mentioned there was another Knuck I was negotiating to buy (yeah, sure!) but I liked his machine and would like to check it out.

That afternoon he let me take it out for a ride. Now, I hadn't ridden a handshifter in two or three years and I was out of practice. But having read about my adventures on my old ex-police, handshifter Shovelhead in *American Iron Magazine,* Tommy was more confident in my riding abilities than I was—especially considering the congestion of Sturgis during the rally. After a half dozen false starts (read, stalling out) in the parking lot and out of the sight of most people, I started to get the hang of it again.

Then, I was out in the overwhelming Sturgis traffic. No matter how crowded the lanes were, when anyone saw me rolling this handsome old dinosaur their way, they would give me the thumbs up and clear a path for me. Good thing, as the old drum brakes offered questionable stopping power. By the time I got back to Tommy I knew I had to own this bike, but I had to keep my excitement to myself or I'd end up paying way too much. I guess I kept a poker face, because Tommy did let it go for a fair price.

I arranged to have the bike shipped to my office in Connecticut where I immediately began to make changes. I tossed the straight pipes for a reproduction of the stock exhaust system, installed a stock Harley solo seat, new Coker whitewall tires, and some cool-looking saddlebags. I rode it locally for a couple of years. Finally, when I got it up almost to 100,000 miles on the odometer, the mechanical problems started: Loss of power, harder to start, and tougher to shift. Now I was planning to ride this bike from *American Iron Magazine*'s Connecticut headquarters to Milwaukee the next summer as part of Harley's 95th anniversary celebration. I figured it was time to tear her down for a freshening up.

I brought the bike to Moroney's Harley-Davidson in Newburgh, New York, for a diagnosis. They reported the tranny was so badly worn it was ready to explode. They also noted all the valves, guides, rings, and pistons were shot. The flywheels were unsalvageable and to quote the chief mechanic, "Other than the cases, cylinders, and heads, there's not much left worth salvaging in this engine." I'd say this old bike had survived the nearly 100,000 miles rather admirably. I have no idea what past owners did or didn't do to maintain the bike, but it worked.

While we had the bottom end apart, we stroked it from 61 inches (EL designation) to the more powerful 74-inch (FL) displacement, and replaced the aftermarket Mikuni carb with a rebuilt original carb. I thought there might be a few readers at *American Iron Magazine* who were as interested in these old Harleys as I was, so we ran a series of articles on how we rebuilt the bike. I was blown away by how popular it was, even with readers who had never even sat on anything older than an Evo. When I got the rebuilt bike back from Moroney's, I knew this bike was a keeper. We were simply getting her prepared for the next 100,000 miles,

The goal was for me to lead a ride from our offices in Connecticut to Harley's offices in Milwaukee on the Knuck. We promoted the ride in *American Iron Magazine* and invited everyone to ride along who could.

I put a couple of thousand miles on the rebuilt

1990 Harley-Davidson FLSTF Fat Boy

Above: *You can call this Harley-Davidson FLSTF a Fat Boy without risking a knuckle sandwich. In fact, the name was one of endearment to Fat Boy riders everywhere. The FLSTF rode on a Softail frame but was outfitted with its very own solid-center disc wheels, shotgun-style pipes, and a horseshoe-shaped oil tank nestled under the seat. Power came from the venerable 80-cubic-inch (1,310-cc) Evolution V2 engine.(Photograph © Andrew Morland)*

1972 Harley-Davidson XR-TT 750

Above: *Harley-Davidson's iron XR-750 was to be the Motor Company's savior on the racing front in 1969 against the rising sun of Japanese motorcycles. But things did not quite work out that way. The iron XRs did not perform up to snuff, and many black-and-orange riders brought their KRs back out of retirement. With the reworked aluminum XR of 1972, however, Harley-Davidson served notice that it meant business, and the XR-750 went on to become one of the winningest motorcycles ever. Wrapped in slippery bodywork, the TT road-race version battled against Triumph and BSA triples as well as Japanese two-strokers on the pavement. This XR-TT was still flying the colors in vintage races at Daytona Speedway in 1996. Owner: Jon Schultz.*
(Photograph © Andrew Morland)

motor and tranny, changing the oil at 500, 1,000, and 2,000 miles. It ran great, and I was getting pretty excited about the three-day ride halfway across the country to Milwaukee. A few weeks before the departure date I went for a ride with my old friend Mike Baldwin, who in a former life was a world-class road racer. Mike, who had also traded in his high-performance import sport bikes for a Harley Shovelhead, gave me an old windshield he had in the basement. I figured out a way to mount it on my Knuck and letter it with "*American Iron*" by hand just as they would have in days gone by. I was pumped.

The day of the big ride we all gathered at the local Harley dealer. There were over one hundred Harleys and several chase vehicles assembled in the sunshine that morning. I was finally going to ride the fifty-one-year-old Harley home to Milwaukee, and it looked like we were going to do it with style.

Before we fired up and headed West that morning, a number of the people planning on riding to Milwaukee with us admired the Knuck. I was amused when several of them complained that the bike would slow them down. I laughed and told them not to worry about it. I expect most of them learned something about old Harleys later that day when I rolled past them on the highway at over 75 mph.

It felt terrific leading over a hundred Harleys heading for their home on the Knuck. That is until the clutch let go in the Pennsylvania mountains mid-afternoon, leaving us stranded on the side of the road. As the other riders rolled on past me, I asked *American Iron Magazine* Editor Chris Maida to lead the ride to the next stop and we'd catch up with them that evening. We pushed the bike onto a chase vehicle trailer and hauled her to that night's planned stop.

We joined up with the crew for dinner then pulled the Knuck into Thunder Harley-Davidson's work area where my friend Chris "Razzle Dazzle" Rasile pulled the old clutch for a look see. The clutch plates in my Knuck looked original. I doubt they could have lasted 100,000 miles, but it made me think about it. Thunder Harley-Davidson didn't stock Knucklehead clutch plates, so we installed Shovelhead plates, which he had in stock. They worked fine. We were in and out in less than two hours.

1940 Harley-Davidson 61 OHV Knucklehead

Legend has it that Harley-Davidson dealers were so thrilled by the first showing of the new 61 OHV model at the November 25, 1935, dealer's convention that one overzealous dealer pulled a pistol and emptied several bullets into the ceiling. The overhead-valve engine was seen as the Motor Company's savior in the dark days of the Great Depression and the ongoing war with arch-rival Indian. Still, it was many months from the unveiling of the new E Series at the dealer's convention until actual production motorcycles graced showroom floors. The new 61-cubic-inch (1,000-cc) V-twin engine fathered 40 hp and pushed the 515-pound (233-kg) motorcycle to a top speed of some 90 mph (144 km/h). Owner: Keith Campbell. (Photograph © Andrew Morland)

Bagger Custom

Above: *This Bagger is such a lowdown Dresser that it doesn't need a kick stand. Built and designed primarily by Terry McConnell, it started life as a cop bike. The frame was stretched 4 inches (10 cm), and rides on 18-inch (46-cm) wheels covered by Arlen Ness Taildragger fenders. Power comes from a hopped-up 80-ci (1,310-cc) Evo motor. Owner: Doug Daniel. (Photograph © Timothy Remus)*

The next morning, I rode out of the shop and got a standing ovation from the other riders, who apparently had assumed the Knuck was out for the count. We were still on schedule and the bike spent less than 200 miles on a trailer.

Those 200 miles were the best weather of the entire ride out; it rained the rest of the way. The closer we got to Milwaukee, the worse it got. Chicago was terrible with the worst possible combination of torrential rain and hail, serious potholes, and the bad fortune of hitting town just in time to enjoy the rush-hour traffic. Several of the riders with us went down, but fortunately no one got hurt. The Knucklehead never missed a beat, even when the bike and I got totally airborne on the infamous Chicago Loop.

We regrouped at Lake Shore Harley-Davidson and soldiered on through the cold and wet. By now, our numbers had swollen to more than two hundred bikes as we gathered more riders on a regular basis. The weather was dreadful: pouring rain, and now it was getting cold. We had been on the road for three days and in

On the road again

With Sturgis, South Dakota, in their sights, these riders keep the throttle open. The Hardtail custom in front is owned, built, and ridden by Terry "Wizard" McConnell. The bike boasts an unsual color treatment with its silver-gray paint scheme and black pipes. Bringing up the rear is the Bagger owned and ridden by Doug Daniel. (Photograph © Timothy Remus)

the rain for more than half of it. I suspect many of those riding with us had never experienced anything like this before and were looking to Chris Maida and me for leadership. Chris and I were just as numb as they were, but we kept pushing on.

Then, starting about an hour outside of Milwaukee, we began seeing people standing out in the cold and rain with signs welcoming us home. Their presence reached through the cold and rain, through the exhaustion of three days on the road, and touched me deep down in my soul in ways I cannot describe. There were little kids and old folks huddled in the rain on the overpasses a full hour outside of Milwaukee. When they heard us coming there would be a flurry of activity to get the signs up. We could see their generous smiles and genuine waves of friendship. They could not know how much their simple actions meant to us. As we got closer to Milwaukee, their numbers increased, swarming over all the overpasses on the highways. They were better for our spirits than anything I could have wished for.

It almost seemed like my old Knucklehead knew it was going home and responded by running better with each mile. When we rolled into our final destination, Hal's Harley-Davidson in Milwaukee, the bike ran better than new. I don't think that there was a single rider that was less than impressed with what can be done with an older Harley.

1994 Harley-Davidson FLHR Road King Classic

Facing page, top: *The Road King lived up to its name. Designed in the great tradition of Harley-Davidson Big Twins, the FLHR was a touring bike that ate up the road, mile after mile, sea to shining sea. The overhead-valve 45-degree Evolution V² engine displaced 82 ci (1,340 cc) and could travel from horizon to horizon with ease. The Classic edition included extra touring gear, such as panniers and a windscreen. (Photograph © Andrew Morland)*

Arlen Ness "Arrow" Custom

Facing page, bottom: *Most of Arlen Ness's bikes are outstanding, but this one looks like it should be in the Museum of Modern Art. Built on a special rubber-mounted Softail frame, the 80-ci (1,310-cc) hot rod Evo motor features Ness billet heads and accessories, an S&S Super E carburetor, and Carl's camshaft. The pipes and fenders were fabricated by Bob "The Mun" Munroe. The House of Kolor red paint was shot by Carl Brouhad. (Photograph © Timothy Remus)*

The bikes and riders were all soaked. We joined the reception party inside the dealership and several of the riders thanked me for arranging for this ride. They were all in awe of my Knucklehead and said so. Many of them also later told me they were brought to tears by this outpouring of warmth by the locals standing out in the rain to meet and greet us as we rolled into town.

I pushed the bike into our chase truck and let it dry off. The next day delivered bright sunshine, and I gave my Knucklehead the thorough cleaning it had earned. It's kind of funny how many people saw the bike during Harley's 95th anniversary celebration and made some comment about it being a trailer queen. If only they only knew what it had been through on the ride out!

The celebration's high point was the parade to the festivities at the Summerfest Grounds. My wife Gail and I got up early to ride over to the VIP area. While warming the bike up at 6:30 A.M., a number of people, including Jay Leno and Willie G. Davidson, stopped by to admire the bike in front of the hotel. From the VIP area, we got a police escort to the front of the parade, which was a good thing as tens of thousands of bikers had literally slept on their bikes at the start of the parade route, just for the privilege of being at the front.

This was such a big deal; the governor of Wisconsin had closed down the interstate highway system around Milwaukee for half a day to accommodate this parade. While I was not able to see every bike in the parade (there were estimates of over 100,000 bikes in it) I suspect mine was the oldest bike in it. And I'm pretty sure, if there was an older machine, it was not ridden as far as mine to get there.

As we inched down the parade route (not an easy thing with a foot clutch), I felt honored. I had ridden this amazing motorcycle halfway across the country to bring it home a half century after it was built. The parade route was packed with hundreds of thousands, and I was delighted with the reactions my old bike generated as we rolled by. I guess the Knucklehead's appeal is as strong as ever.

Chapter 4

Daredevilry

"Kids, don't try this at home!"
—Famous circus sideshow warning

After reading one too many *Superman* comic books, a certain young motorcyclist began having visions of himself as a miniature Man of Steel. On a fine yet fateful day, he dressed in his best homemade super-hero suit, complete with cape, jumped aboard his Cushman motor scooter, laid flat on the seat like Superman in flight, and blasted off down the street faster than a speeding bullet. Unfortunately, that's not the advised way to ride a cycle, and gravity quickly brought him down to Earth.

Certain folk simply have daredevilry in their blood. Hand some people a Harley, and they head off to chase the sunset. Hand others the same cycle, and they just naturally have to see how far they can wheelie it or jump it.

Hell-bent for leather, 1940s
One of famed cycling daredevil Lucky Lee Lott's Hell Drivers ducks his head, holds his breath, and goes for broke in crashing through a flaming board wall. (Lucky Lee Lott archives)

Hell Driving

By Lucky Lee Lott

"Lucky" Lee Lott began crashing motorcycles and automobiles at state and county fairs around the United States in 1935. In those days, the motorcycle was a relatively new kid on the block, and people thronged to Lott's shows to be wowed by his derring-do. By the 1950s, his Hell Drivers spectacle was famous in all corners of the continent.

He wrote of his lifetime of achievements in his rollicking 1994 memoir *The Legend of the Lucky Lee Lott Hell Drivers*, telling the tales of his most famous stunts: The time he jumped a car into a lake, only to have it sink to the bottom and settle in three feet of muddy silt with him inside. The time he crashed a Ford Tri-Motor airplane into a house, only to have the plane keep on flying out of control off through the countryside and into a barn. The time he lost his hearing during a dynamite-fueled stunt. And the time in 1942 he set a world record by jumping 169 feet (52 m) in an old Ford and re-arranged his back forever after.

These days, Lott is retired in Tampa, Florida, where he has a personal museum of old stunt cars and a scrapbook filled with memorabilia of the good old days crashing cycles and cars.

For more than two decades, I made my living crashing motorcycles. As the leader of Lucky Lee Lott's Hell Drivers, my boys and I laid to eternal rest 17,981 motorcycles and automobiles at county and state fairs throughout the United States and Canada. Not only did our gasoline opera feature a blood-curdling blend of daredevilry and stunts, we also destroyed more fine machinery in more imaginative ways than you ever dreamed possible.

It all began in 1935 when I was twenty years old. I had a stash of loot from selling vacuum cleaners and so I decided to spread my wings and get into the daredevil business.

I didn't have a resumé to handle such endeavors as stunt driving but I did have other qualifications, to wit: I was a salesman, for evidence look at my vacuum cleaner savings. I could act in front of people and had been with the circus at one time. I liked to do daring things, such as my high-diving job at the Chicago World's Fair. And I had a gift of gab. Who needs a resumé with qualifications like that?

I had grand dreams of crashing cycles and cars in front of adoring crowds, so I gathered several of my buddies around the kitchen table—including my fourteen-year-old brother Neal and his lifelong friend Lou "Batter" Crooks—and began making plans. The first thing we needed was a name. "Satan's Pals" had a ring to it, even if it was slightly incongruous. We plotted to paint our cars and motorcycles pale white as though they were cemetery ghosts; our new moniker would be written in garish red, dripping down like fresh blood.

Satan's Pals. A daredevilry stunt show full of

Hell driving, 1940s
Hell Driver Rocky Decker jumps his Harley through a wall of flames as the crowd holds its collective breath. (Lucky Lee Lott archives)

chills, thrills, and spills. We would play every county fair in the state of Illinois. It was just what the fans wanted—even though they didn't know it. Yet.

Now we needed some cars to wreck. I bought two crashed Fords from a junkyard—a Tudor that was half burnt out but still ran, and a Fordor that had been rolled. Batter was handy with a sledgehammer, so he got to work and punched the roof back out on the four-door. Then he lit up his welding torch and added in some reinforcing pipes and welded all of the doors shut. This was going to be the fledgling outfit's "roll car." Batter had his Harley-Davidson that would come in handy for jumps, and I had a DeSoto Airflow that could also be put to use.

I got permission from a local farmer to use his pasture for practice, and Satan's Pals started learning how to be daredevils the hard way. Using a 6-foot (1.8-m) length of baling wire wrapped in a leather jacket as a safety belt, we practiced rolling our roll car. On his first attempt, Batter actually got it to roll twice—although the second roll was accidental, and he wound up face down in the dirt. His carefully considered comment afterward was, "That's like doing a high dive without any water in the pool."

In truth, doing stunts like that without ramps was like a carpenter building a house without a hammer. So, at night, I put the kitchen table back to work as a drafting board and designed ramps and blocks for jumping our cycles and cars; the design I created in those first days of Satan's Pals remained the exact design during my full tenure of daredevil business for the next twenty years. During the days, I drove around town with a speaker mounted to the roof of my newly painted DeSoto announcing the debut show on the Fourth of July, promising "Thrills, spills, and free parking." The crew kept on practicing, earning our degree in daredevilry from the school of hard knocks.

Each of the Pals had the opportunity to try their hand with the roll car in practice. That poor vehicle suffered—oh, how it suffered! With Batter as our mechanic, we took all the tools we could scrounge out to that farmer's field to keep the cars alive, everything from pliers to screwdrivers to our trusty sledgehammer. We collected lumber off of scrap billboards to build ramps and walls to crash through.

People gathered from miles around to watch these strange goings-on. Some were so fascinated they even

donated cars for us to practice on.

We had a method, and so now my motivation was to get somewhere to debut the show.

A daredevil show like Satan's Pals couldn't get onto a fairgrounds or racetrack because I didn't have an insurance policy backing me up. So I took a ride out of town and found a farmer's field that we could rent. The farmer and his family even offered to help sell tickets.

I set up shop, had posters and handbills printed, and found a junkyard that would let us have six cars for $1.25 each—that's one dollar and twenty-five cents apiece! The junker even delivered the cars.

All we needed now was binder twine and pieces of cloth to tart up our field, control the crowds, and delineate a race course in the pasture. The crew got to work and we hauled the cars over from the airport across the road. I had brought along a roll of 500 tickets, which we hoped to use all of. Kids were free.

I had a portable typewriter and worked on things to say, jokes and that sort of stuff. I didn't want to forget the commercials for the people who bought newspaper space and had their names on our advertising: the local shops for Standard Oil, Goodyear Tires, and the like.

The crew had everything in order. We lay down in the shade of the junkers and sacked out. We had put in some hard labor.

The day of the show finally arrived. The farmer's family came over and I gave them nail aprons packed with tickets and change money and they went off over the rise to the highway to handle something they knew nothing about.

The show was set for 2 P.M. I had music on the turntable at 1:00, and there we waited, hoping someone would come see us. Our site being in a small valley, we naturally couldn't see the highway in either direction but heard a horn once in a while.

At 1:30, I looked up and here came an Illinois Highway State Trooper walking across to my car.

"Who runs this outfit?" Bull Moose asked.

My voice never cracked as it did on the Fourth of July 1935.

"I'll have to take the blame, but we're waiting for customers."

Bull Moose responded, "If you'd open that gate, I'll help you get them in."

What?

A job well done, 1941
The happy Hell Drivers congratulate each other on surviving another 60-mph (97-kph) head-on crash stunt. From left, daredevil clown Happy Maxwell, cycle jumper Rocky Decker, and last but not least, the one and only Lucky Lee Lott. (Lucky Lee Lott archives)

"You've got a backup of traffic four miles to the light in Kewanee and five miles down to Route 91. Let's get with it."

Out of sight and out of mind over the hill from the pasture, we had forgotten to open the gate! Route 34 was a national route and four lanes at that. It was packed with cars as far as the eye could see. But the cars weren't blocking the traffic—everyone was headed for the show. The 500 tickets didn't last long. "Just take the money," I called out to our crew and the farmer's family, all working feverishly to get the crowd into the pasture.

At 3 P.M., I put the "Comedian's Gallop" on the turntable, and with apologies to all, the show swung into action. We kicked off the first Satan's Pals show with The Two-Wheel Drive. I drove my DeSoto onto a ramp and lifted two wheels off the ground, piloting

it the length of the pasture. We did The Slide For Life with a daredevil hanging off the rear bumper, sliding along behind the car at 50 mph through a patch of burning gasoline. Then The Human Battering Ram with our man laid head-forward on the hood of the Ford while another drove him through a board wall set aflame. Batter did a motorcycle board wall crash along with some precision driving. And there was The Ski Wall where a car was jumped off a 2-foot-high ramp and through a blazing wall.

Then came the Blindfold Jump.

The crowd waited in silent anticipation as Batter sat astride his Harley while I tied a blindfold around his helmetless head. He kicked the V-twin to life, gassed it a couple times, and then rooster-tailed down the pasture. He took one quick peak from under the blindfold to make certain he had the Milwaukee Marvel lined up right, and then gunned the engine. He came roaring past the crowd and onto the 7.5-foot-high (2.3-m) wooden ramp that sent him soaring through the air to crash into a burning wall of wood and excelsior. The flames engulfed him as he split through the wall with his head tucked down like a battering ram. Batter and his Harley landed and bounced a couple times.

But something felt wrong: The cycle was on fire.

Feeling a bit warm, Batter abandoned the flaming Harley at full throttle and dove—still blindfolded—for the safety of the alfalfa. The riderless cycle careened down the field afire until it tipped over and flipped. Another Pal rushed to the scene with a bucket of water.

When a bent and charred Batter struggled to his feet and threw off his blindfold, the crowd went crazy.

A show was born.

From that day forward, I gained the nickname "Lucky," and the show soon changed its moniker to the Hell Drivers. I used my take from that first show to buy gas and bologna sandwiches, and we started

touring the United States and Canada. By the late 1940s, the Lucky Lee Lott Hell Drivers was the largest daredevil show in the world.

We jumped cars into lakes, drove Ford Tri-Motor airplanes into houses, and I set a world record in 1942 by jumping a car 169 feet (51.5 m). They were tricks that needed more than just bottled courage. A top-notch motorcycle daredevil required three essential components: balance, bravery, and continence.

Many years before the advent of the motorcycle, the poet Sir Walter Scott framed the words that I have lived by in his poem "The Last Minstrel": "The will to do and the soul to dare." These are words that still dwell in my head at this ripe old age of eighty-four after surviving many a bone-jarring, back-bending, heart-halting motorcycle stunt.

We daredevils were true engineers. In the Hell Drivers, we took pride in crashing motorcycles through brick walls, wooden walls, tin walls, and walls that were set aflame. We drove motorcycles head-on into speeding automobiles, jumped from motorcycles onto airplanes at 80 mph, and leaped motorcycles into bodies of water. Daredevilry was a science. It was not foolhardiness or merely the libidinous nature of young men, for broken bones, lacerations, and bruises were not badges of honor among professional daredevils.

Forty years later, I still have fond memories of my signature stunt, the Tin Wall Crash, wherein I piloted a motorcycle through a wall of nothing less than 28-gauge furnace metal. The trick was to fit a sharp blade to the front wheel's fender and stake down the tin wall as taut as possible. Then I just gassed the throttle, aimed straight, and ducked my head. Back in those days, we wore football helmets to keep our craniums in one piece.

I also parlayed my knack of crashing motorcycles into a sideline career as a movie stunt man—"fall guys," as we called them for obvious reasons. I did my bit in Marlon Brando's *The Wild One* as well as many other movies. Guys who could crash cycles and cars without getting hurt and running up the hospital bill were in demand in Hollywood.

Baton-twirling daredevil
Steady balance and a strong bungee cord were the keys to leading the local Fourth of July parade from atop a Harley.

Bob Drone Custom

When California Harley dealer Bob Drone set out to build a new custom he had two goals: "I wanted to show people what you could do with genuine Harley-Davidson parts, and I wanted to utilize the talents of Steve Moal, a very talented craftsman who does much of the metal work on my cars and bikes." What Bob described and Steve formed is an unusual Harley Softail with a hot-rod soul. The cycle was made up of hand-formed fenders and body panels formed from sheet aluminum in Steve's shop. Instead of welding the bike together and grinding the welds to make them invisible, the bike is held together with rivets—lots of rivets. Rather than paint the panels, Bob chose to leave them in raw aluminum, polished to a high luster. (Photograph © Timothy Remus)

In my three decades of daredevilry, we went through a lot of front forks and other front-end components. We also went through a lot of motorcycles, period. The Hell Drivers typically bought our cycles from finance companies that had repossessed the bikes from their "owners." We also picked up crashed cycles on the cheap from insurance companies, sorted out the good parts, and made one cycle out of two, or three, or four.

The best motorcycle I ever used for the Head-On Crash was a Henderson Four, which we tracked down once upon a time. The Henderson was just built well. It was something solid and dependable beneath you when you lined up against a speeding car for the Head-On.

One of my motorcycle stuntmen, Joe Langford, had an English-built Ariel Red Hunter for a time, and that was a good cycle for balancing acts. We also once found a 1947 Ariel Square Four up in Canada, and my riders Steve Stiles and Ron Childers used it for their acts for several years. That Ariel was a delightful machine.

One of our favorite cycles was the Indian Scout. Wall of Death riders loved it for their circus and fair sideshows for the same reasons we did: The Scout was lightweight yet perfectly balanced. The chassis was set up just right, but above all, the Indian's V-twin engine was balanced, nearly vibrationless, and simply kept on ticking despite all of the Human Battering Rams, Flaming Wall Crashes, and Ten-Car Jumps. It was the ideal machine for a head stand.

But our workhorse cycles were Harleys, Milwaukee's finest. It's what we started with at our first show on the Fourth of July 1935. Forever after, I always kept my eye out for a Harley-Davidson, and performed many a stunt on that good Wisconsin Iron.

The Wall of Death

The Wall of Death is an all-American marriage of motorcycles, P. T. Barnum–style showmanship, and death-defying daredevilry. Take a large barrellike chamber with high walls that create a never-ending vertical road, and drive a cycle around the inside at top speed.

Build it, and folks will come. For decades now, people at state and county fairs throughout the United States have anted up their hard-earned cash to be dazzled by the spectacle and deafened by the contained roar of the machine.

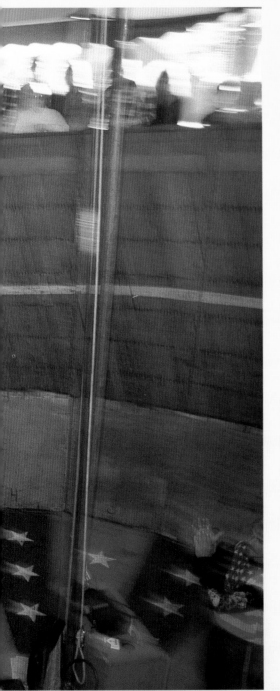

"Suicide Club"
Right: *Thrills aplenty were promised by this Wall of Death and stunt-riding poster.*

"Chills, thrills & spills"
Above: *A traveling Wall of Death show rouses the crowd for another display of cycling derring-do. Sadly, many surviving Wall of Death shows opt to perform on cheap and lightweight Japanese cycles; this show stands tall behind its bevy of "genuine" Harleys. (Photograph © Jerry Irwin)*

Riding the wall
Left: *A Harley-mounted rider "gets dizzy" circling a Wall of Death. (Photograph © Jerry Irwin)*

Evel Ways

By Evel Knievel

Robert Craig "Evel" Knievel was an all-American hero like no other. At a time in the 1960s and 1970s when the country was splitting apart in a million directions, Evel Knievel was pursuing his own personal American dream: living dangerously by his wits, challenging the authority of gravity, crafting P. T. Barnum–style spectacle. He was a self-made man earning the American Dream in the most outrageous manner ever dreamed possible. He was John Wayne on wheels, a daredevil Elvis, Bogart with a helmet, JFK with pointy sideburns, an original.

Evel Knievel earned his sobriquet while stealing hubcaps in his hometown of Butte, Montana, when a victim hollered after him, "You're a little evil, Knievel." The moniker stuck and became a household name around the world.

These remembrances of motorcycles past come from the closest thing Knievel has done in terms of writing an autobiography. *Evel Ways: The Attitude of Evel Knievel* was published in 1999 and is chock full of stories, quotes, photographs, and memorabilia.

When I was a kid, I had an old BSA Bantam 125 my dad bought for me. I was doing wheelies and other stunts at an early age, and also rode a Honda.

I rode a Norton 750 Commando when I started jumping, sponsored by Mike Berliner and his brother, Joe. Then I rode a Triumph but I couldn't get along with the distributor. It was a beautiful 650-cc bike, a T120 Bonneville.

Just before the Caesars Palace jump, I decided to cash in on some favors. I had loads of trouble with Johnson Motors out of California. They provided the Triumph motorcycle for me—one of the best motorcycles built—but did nothing in return for all the promoting I did for them. I threatened Pete Coleman, who was the president, that if he didn't put an attorney on the next plane to Las Vegas with a $20,000 check, the Triumph would miss so badly that it would make it the laughing stock of the motorcycle world. I told him I'd burn his cycle in front of Caesars Palace. Can you believe he accused me of blackmail?

But you better believe they sent that attorney and he had that check. I still have the motorcycle from that jump.

Then I rode the American Eagle. The American Eagle was imported from [Laverda of] Italy and introduced to me by Jack McCormack and Walt Fulton. When Jack was [part] of American Honda Motor Company, he coined the phrase, "You meet the nicest people on a Honda." He is solely responsible for

Evel Knievel, 1970s

From a volatile boyhood to ice-hockey star, ace insurance salesman to motorcycle daredevil, Evel Knievel embodied the American Dream. He was unique among heroes: He was a living, breathing Superman, able to leap a lineup of Mack trucks in a single bound. These days, the Evel legend still looms, kept alive by his own website, www.evel.com. (Photograph from Evel and Kelly Knievel)

the success of Honda in America.

Harley-Davidson sponsored me and paid me the money I needed to continue jumping. The Harley-Davidson XR-750 had so much torque that when I took off at 70 to 85 miles per hour the bike would twist in the air.

The people at Harley-Davidson were one of the finest families I ever did business with. They kept their word and stood by my side the eight years I worked with them. I was proud to be a part of the Harley-Davidson team.

Now I ride a custom bike built for me by California Motorcycle Company, a division of Indian Motorcycle Company of Gilroy, California. It's a limited-edition Evel Knievel Signature series with painted graphics and gold-plated accents that depict my famous jumps and crashes.

Yet another broken record . . .

This poster from the Ontario Motor Speedway in California bid all motorcycle fans to watch their hero break yet another record, this time jumping no less than nineteen Dodges. Over the years, the daredevil records fell like bowling pins beneath Evel Knievel's cycle.

"Color me lucky."
—Evel Knievel

Evel lunchbox

Evel Knievel was probably the only motorcycle hero to be stamped in metal on children's lunchboxes. This well-used and well-loved lunchbox dates from the 1970s, Evel's heyday.

Catching up on history

Dedicated Motor Company scholars do their homework on Harley history at the York, Pennsylvania, factory museum. The object of today's lesson is a 1936 Knucklehead. (Photograph © Jerry Irwin)

Chapter 5

Legends

*"Je n'ai pas besoin personne
au Harley-Davidson."*
—Brigitte Bardot

———————————

The legend that is Harley-Davidson has attracted other legends. Clark Gable had one. Roy Rogers owned many. Elvis Presley bought a new one almost every year. Brigitte Bardot sang perhaps the first song of freedom about them: When she rode her Harley, she didn't need anyone else.

Harleys also starred in countless films, from *The Wild One* to *The Wild Angels* and beyond. And after the movie credits rolled, the line between life and art became blurred as many actors rode Harleys in real life or the celluloid cycles influenced folk to build their own replicas.

These essays examine the aura surrounding some of the most famous events in Harley pop culture.

Riding buddies, 1930s
Members of the Calgary Motorcycle Club enjoy an outing in Canada's Banff National Park. The Harley on the left is accompanied by a British Francis Barnett cycle. (Provincial Archives of Alberta)

Once Upon a Time in the Wild West

By Michael Dregni

Michael Dregni is the author of several obscure books on a variety of esoteric subjects. Among others, he has authored an engineering history of Ferrari automobiles, *Inside Ferrari*, two pop-culture histories of motor scooters, and two motorcycling histories published by Voyageur Press, *The Spirit of the Motorcycle* and *Harley-Davidson Collectibles*.

This essay, adapted from *The Spirit of the Motorcycle*, looks at one of the formative events in creating motorcycling's outlaw mystique.

 It was a movie with a reputation, as folk used to say in the old days about a "fallen" woman or a teenage juvenile delinquent.

I remember the first time I saw it, almost four decades after it was first released. It was showing at a revival theater that screened an oddball assortment of classics and forgotten movies from days past. The theater was as old as many of the movies themselves and indeed had shown some of them when they first opened. The red velvet that covered the chairs was threadbare, the seats squeaked when you sat down, and the air had the smell of popcorn from decades ago. Then, the lights dimmed and the surroundings were forgotten. Onto the screen in glorious black and white burst the opening images of a country road and the sound of motorcycles in the distance. In a flash, the title rolled across the screen: *The Wild One*.

Although decades had passed since its debut, there was still an aura to this famous—or more likely, infamous—film. It was dangerous, subversive. It even began with a warning that echoed the first lines of Dante's guided tour of Hell: "This is a shocking story. It could never take place in most American towns—but it did in this one. It is a public challenge not to let it happen again."

It was a day that would live in infamy. Pearl Harbor was history and World War II was finally finished, but in the days after the war, some young men returning from battle had a craving for something different from the ordered life and the American dream that they had fought for. Kickstarting a motorcycle into life and riding off to find the horizon filled the bill. It was just such a ride that brought a group of motorcyclists searching for fun to the sleepy little town of Hollister, California, on the Fourth of July in 1947.

What really happened at Hollister is impossible to tell from today's vantage. There are many versions of the story of the day that changed motorcycling forever, and none of them are consistent with each other. There's one thing they all agree on, however: The story as presented in *Life* magazine and Marlon

Chino
Lee Marvin was Chino in The Wild One, *the leader of the gang of* bad *bad guys who follows on the wheels of Marlon Brando's* good *bad guys in coming to terrorize the town.*

Brando's movie, *The Wild One*, was a hoax.

It all began with a photograph. Late editions of the San Francisco *Chronicle* on July 5, 1947, carried the first version of the story: A gang of drunken motorcyclists called the Boozefighters had invaded the town of Hollister on America's most sacrosanct day, July 4. They had raced through the streets on their motorized steeds, terrifying good people. They drank beer and brawled and distressed young damsels. Life in Hollister would never be the same.

A single photograph was sent out over the wires to news media around the country. In the photograph taken by Barney Petersen, a fat slob of a motorcyclist sat astride his Harley, surrounded by a sea of empty bottles. He clutched a couple beers in his evil claws and leered at the camera. In his eyes was a cold message: "Bar your doors and lock away your daughters because I'm coming to get you."

A photo editor at *Life* saw the photograph and marked it for use. At the time, *Life* held the respect of Americans like no magazine before or since. *Life* had told the awful story of World War II in words and photographs like Grandpa sitting down to spin a yarn in front of the fireplace after a turkey dinner with all the dressings. It was not until Walter Cronkite arrived in American living rooms every evening on the television that the news media had a more powerful single voice.

Life reported: "On the Fourth of July weekend, 4,000 members of a motorcycle club roared into Hollister, California, for a three-day convention. They quickly tired of ordinary motorcycle thrills and turned to more exciting stunts. Racing their vehicles down the main streets and through traffic lights, they rammed into restaurants and bars, breaking furniture and mirrors . . . police arrested many . . . but could not restore order."

When *Life* ran the photo with the story of the Hollister brouhaha, the awful event was catapulted into the hearts and minds of Americans everywhere. The story of Hollister had all the makings of myth. It was the modern western, with the lawless men in black riding into town to confront the good citizenry, only to be banished by a duel with the fearless lawman. It was like a glorified war movie, a blitzkrieg by minions of the evil empire upon the peace-loving townspeople. Almost overnight, a new menace was

at hand, and every motorcyclist was suddenly seen as one of the dreaded Boozefighters.

Then came the movie. In 1953, *The Wild One* starring Marlon Brando opened at a theater near you. Producer Stanley Kramer and director Laslo Benedek knew a good story when they saw one. They jumped on the Hollister incident, read the news accounts, shook their heads once more at the photograph, and fashioned a fictionalized account of the event.

In the film, Marlon Brando played the leader of the Black Rebels Motorcycle Club, a cool cat named Johnny Strabler who wore a black leather jacket like a suit of armor against the world. Atop his Triumph Thunderbird, he led his gang on a Fourth of July ride up the California coast, stopping to wreak havoc at a motorcycle race before moving on to terrorize an innocent small town based on Hollister.

An early scene provided a quick Hollywood-style sociological analysis of the roots of postwar disaffection that gave birth to motorcycle gangs. A highway patrolman who had just chased away Brando's gang warns another officer.

"Where'd that bunch come from?" an officer asks, playing the devil's advocate for a theater full of moviegoers asking themselves the same question.

"I don't know," responds the other patrolman, the voice of all-knowing wisdom. "Everywhere. I don't even think they know where they're going. Nutty. Ten guys like that gives people the idea everybody that drives a motorcycle is crazy. What are they trying to prove?"

"Beats me," answers the first officer, the voice of the common people. "Looking for somebody to push them around so they can get sore and show how tough they are."

When the gang arrives in town, it makes a beeline for Bleeker's Cafe and Bar. Members drop their change into the jukebox and order up rounds of beer. One townsgirl, taken by the excitement that follows the gang, says, "Black Rebels Motorcycle Club, that's cute! Hey Johnny, what are you rebelling against?"

With studied nonchalance, Johnny answered, "Whaddya got?"

He further explained his philosophy of life to the waitress named Cathy, played by Mary Murphy. She is curious about Johnny and his gang, and queries him: "Where are you going when you leave here?

The Wild One poster

These days, The Wild One is considered a classic, but when it was first released in 1953, it was a box office flop. Few folk wanted to see a film about motorcycle gangs—especially one in which the "bad" guy was actually kind of a good guy, an anti-hero. In the days of westerns and war movies where the good guys wore white and the bad guys were in black, a black-leather-jacketed good guy seemed all wrong.

The Hell's Angels come to town

Mention of a friendly little motorcycle club in California called the "Hell's Angels" was made in the Motor Company's owner's magazine The Enthusiast in the late 1930s. Following World War II, the Hell's Angels were back. They were born like many before them as a motorcycling club made up of former servicemen tasting freedom after World War II. Originally based in the San Francisco–Oakland Bay Area, their image grew along with their disaffection from society. (Photograph © Jerry Irwin)

Don't you know?"

Johnny: "We're just gonna go."

Cathy: "Just trying to make conversation; it means nothing to me."

Johnny: "Look, on weekends, we go out and have a ball."

Cathy: "What do you do? I mean, do you just ride around, or do you go on some sort of picnic or something?"

Johnny: "A picnic? Man, you are too square! I have to straighten you out. Now listen, you don't go any one special place, that's cornball style. You just go!" he says to a snap of his fingers. "A bunch gets together after a week. It builds up. The idea is to have a ball. Now, if you gonna stay cool you gotta wail. You gotta put something down. You gotta make some jive, don't you know what I'm talking about?"

Obviously, she doesn't have a clue.

Soon, Johnny will take Cathy for a ride on his Triumph, giving society a taste of freedom on two wheels. "I've never ridden on a motorcycle before," Cathy exclaims with delight. "It's fast. It scared me. But I forgot everything. It felt good."

Then, the true bad guy shows his face. Lee Marvin and his gang of *bad* bad guys ride into town. As Cathy walks home from work, Marvin on his Harley-Davidson leads his gang to encircle the woman, spinning around in a kaleidoscope of revving bikes moving in for the kill—just like the Indians circling the

wagon train in a Wild West shoot-'em-up. Only Johnny can save her, whisking her away on his Triumph like a knight in shining armor.

Brando's character was confusing to 1950s audiences. He was the bad guy and the good guy at the same time. This didn't make sense: Everyone knew full well that the bad guys wore black hats and the good guys wore white. It was repeated every Saturday matinee in the horse opera at the local theater.

Now, suddenly, here was Johnny wearing a black leather jacket and a black cap, terrorizing a town with his good-for-nothing bikers—and then midway through the movie another side of his character gradually comes to light. Johnny ain't all bad. Just confused. Under the mask of that emotionless face and the armor of his jacket, he's introspective, questioning, maybe as confused about his direction in life as the audience is confused about his character. Johnny was the first anti-hero role in Hollywood.

Marlon Brando had the look down pat. "The part was actor-proof," he wrote forty years later in his autobiography, *Songs My Mother Taught Me*. That may have been a self-deprecating brag, or perhaps Brando didn't realize that in many ways he *was* Johnny.

Brando provided his own psychoanalysis of Johnny: "More than most parts I've played in the movies or onstage, I related to Johnny, and because of this, I believe I played him as more sensitive and sympathetic than the script envisioned. There's a line in the picture where he snarls, 'Nobody tells *me* what to do.' That's exactly how I've felt all my life. Like Johnny, I have always resented authority. I have been constantly discomfited by people

Mike McAllister Custom
Here is a project that started out simple and then got simply out of hand. Builder Mike McAllister crafted a Softail with extra rake and stretch and an X-drive swing-arm kit to stuff in the monster 200x16 Avon rear tire on PM billet rims. Power comes from a hot-rod 80-ci (1,310-cc) Evo motor. Owner: Tom Rose. (Photograph © Timothy Remus)

telling me what to do, and have always thought that Johnny took refuge in his lifestyle because he was wounded—that he'd had little love as a kid and was trying to survive the emotional insecurity that his childhood had forced him to carry into adulthood. Because of the emotional pain of feeling like a nobody, he became arrogant and adopted a pose of indifference to criticism. He did everything to appear strong when inside he was soft and vulnerable and fought hard to conceal it. He had lost faith in the fabric of society and had made his own world. He was a rebel, but a strong part of him was sensitive and tender. At the time I told a reporter that 'I wanted to show that gentleness and tolerance is the only way to dissipate the forces of social destruction' because I view Johnny as a man torn by an inner struggle beyond his capacity to express it. He had been so disappointed in life that it was difficult for him to express love, but beneath his hostility lay a desperate yearning and desire to feel love because he'd had so little of it. I could have just as easily been describing myself. It seemed perfectly natural for me to play this role."

The movie was not a hit when it made its debut. Many theater-owners refused to screen such trash; others who dared to were read the riot act by do-gooders. "The public's reaction to *The Wild One* was, I believe, a product of its time and circumstances," Brando wrote. "It was only seventy-nine minutes long, short by modern standards, and it looks dated and corny now; I don't think it has aged well. But it became a kind of cult film."

The film struck a chord with a certain disaffected crowd that were tantalized by the rebellion—and by Brando's character. He was a romanticized Robin Hood on a cycle, offering would-be rebels an image to live by. Sales of black leather jackets soared, Brando related in his autobiography, and suddenly became a symbol, although what the symbol stood for was not truly understood. It was the dawn of the juvenile delinquent craze, a horror mirrored in numerous paperback potboiler novels and Hollywood films. A new star was born riding on the wave of this craze, a young actor named James Dean, who in his film *A Rebel Without a Cause* came to stand against everything society stood for.

Brando writes that he never expected *The Wild*

One to have such an impact: "I was as surprised as anyone when T-shirts, jeans and leather jackets suddenly became symbols of rebellion. In the film there was a scene in which somebody asked my character, Johnny, what I was rebelling against, and I answered, *"Whaddya got?"* But none of us involved in the picture ever imagined it would instigate or encourage youthful rebellion. . . .

"After *The Wild One* was finished, I couldn't look at it for weeks; when I did, I didn't like it because I thought it was too violent."

Reading between the lines of Brando's autobiography, it seems obvious that *The Wild One* also played an important role in changing Brando's life, whether he realized it or not.

"I never knew that there were sleeping desires and feelings in our society whose buttons would be hit so uncannily in that film. In hindsight, I think people responded to the movie because of the budding social and cultural currents that a few years later exploded volcanically on college campuses and the streets of America. Right or wrong, we were at the beginning of a new era after several years of transition following World War II; young people were beginning to doubt and question their elders and to challenge their values, morals and the established institutions of authority. There was a wisp of steam just beneath the surface when we made that picture. Young people looking for a reason—any reason—to rebel. I simply happened to be at the right place at the right time in the right part—and I also had the appropriate state of mind for the role."

John Cameron was there at Hollister on the Fourth of July, 1947. He was a founding member of the Boozefighters, a ringleader on two wheels. He remembers the events that created the myth and calls it all a hoax.

Cameron spent the best years of his life aboard a motorcycle. In a 1995 videotaped interview with motorcycle historian Paul Johnson, he read his resumé: "I been riding motorcycles since 1928. I've had pretty near Harleys all my life—except one Crocker, which is the only bike I bought new, and I still have it."

The Boozefighters were not exactly a knitting circle, but on the other hand they weren't overgrown

Bikers

In 1958, Jerry Irwin was discharged from the Army and went straight out to buy himself a motorcycle. He began riding with some friends in Pennsylvania and New Jersey, and while they were out on their bikes, he snapped photographs—the start of another new hobby.

Jerry's photos of friends in the Pagans and Warlocks motorcycle clubs offer candid portraits and documentary images of bikers in the mid-1960s. As he described them, "They were a bunch of nice guys trying to have a good time."

These images also led to a career for Jerry as a full-time photographer. He has not forsaken his motorcycle, however, and ventures annually to the rallies in Sturgis, South Dakota, and Daytona Beach, Florida.

Boy Scouts that had turned world-class delinquents either. In Cameron's mind, they were a bunch of good old boys who liked beer and bikes, just like members of the other motorcycle clubs starting up around that same time in California—the 13 Rebels, Yellow Jackets, Galloping Gooses, Hell's Angels. Most of them were former servicemen who were drawing $20 a week for the first year out of the service—the so-called 52/20 benefit—and they were eager to taste some of the freedom they had been fighting for. But as another Boozefighter said, "We never tried to hurt anybody, because we'd all been hurt in the war. Believe me, baby, all of us had suffered in that war."

Cameron related the origin of the Boozefighters: "You've heard of 'Wino Willie'?" he starts in his best grandma-telling-a-fairy-tale-to-grandchildren voice. "He was a good friend of mine." One day, just after World War II had ended, Wino Willie Forkner, Cameron, and some other buddies were spectating at a Class C race at El Cajon, California. "We were out in the parking lot, and that crazy Willie said, 'Let's put on a show!'

"Willie went riding right through the crash wall during intermission. The flag man tried to wave him off, but Willie ran right by him," Cameron related, a happy, misty-eyed look coming into his eyes at the memory. Astride his Indian Chief, Willie roared off down the straightaway at full throttle in full view of the abhorring crowd. "I thought he wasn't going to make that turn because I knew he was drunk," Cameron said. Lo and behold, Willie made the turn and blasted around the track for another lap—until he augured in while careening through a different turn. "He tried to get back up again, but I ran out and pulled the two spark plug wires off his bike.

"Then here comes the law, and Willie went to jail," Cameron continued.

Willie was let loose again in ninety days, and that's when the Boozefighters got kickstarted.

"Willie belonged to a club called the 13 Rebels," said Cameron. "He went to a club meeting [after he got out of jail], and they jumped all over him about what he done. So he ripped his sweater off and quit."

Cameron and his bunch were having a beer at their chosen corner of heaven, the All American Bar in South Los Angeles, when the rebellious Willie walked in, stripped of his 13 Rebels colors. "We were

"Our way of life"
The T-shirt says it all. (Photograph © Jerry Irwin)

sitting there drinking a little," remembered Cameron, "and Willie said we should start our own club." Someone retorted, "Yeah, but what'll we call it?" Another, well-oiled motorcyclist named Walt Porter drawled out, "Call it the Booozefighters: That's what they're mad about, your boozing and fighting."

It had a certain ring to it. Boozefighters it was.

On the other hand, the name was not exactly custom-made for public relations value, as Cameron remembered: "When that name came out, boy, we was nothing. Other clubs really looked down upon us."

Alongside Wino Willie, Cameron, and the veteran drinker, the Boozefighters were primarily made up of racers. Among the racers were two brothers, Ernie and John Roccio, who would become champion Class A speedway riders in Europe. In the 1950s, the Boozefighters collaborated to build "The Brute," a tuned Harley that peaked at 227 mph on the Bonneville Salt Flats, ridden at different times by Bobby Kelton and Jim Hunter. Meanwhile, Cameron's brother, Jim, won the grueling Big Bear Run desert race. Cameron himself ran TTs, scrambles, and anything else where he was allowed to twist his throttle wide open. Their uniform was a white sweater with green sleeves, a far cry from Brando's black leather jacket.

On the 1947 Fourth of July weekend in question, the Boozefighters made up their minds to hit the road. With visions dancing in their heads of motorcycle races followed by a cold beer, they rode north out of San Diego, bedrolls strapped to the back of their bikes. Hollister appeared before them like an oasis on the never-ending road, so they turned into town and made a beeline for the local watering hole.

"All that mess never happened," Cameron said, shaking his head at memories of the *Life* photograph and *The Wild One*. On the other hand, just as Marlon Brando would say in the movie, it wasn't exactly a picnic outing, either. "Nothing happened that didn't happen at other meets," Cameron continued. "We drank a lot, maybe someone rode their motorcycle into a bar, stuff like that."

Reports differ dramatically about the number of bikers that descended on Hollister and the subsequent goings on. Some say there were upwards of 4,000 motorcyclists swarming through town, racing in the Independence Day hillclimb and scrambles, drag racing down main street, and doing everything from pioneering the art of riding motorcycles through crowded bars to razzing the vestal virgin baton-twirlers in the Independence Day parade.

News of the escapades spread, and somehow a photo was snapped that made the Boozefighters—and all cyclists everywhere—infamous.

"The war was over and *Life* magazine didn't have anything exciting," Cameron recounts, "and so they imported those people [to set up that photograph]. It was an actor. He looked like a Boozefighter named 'Fat Boy' Nelson, but it wasn't him because Fat Boy was riding a Crocker at that time [and the guy in the photo was on a Harley]."

Still, that pictured Harley had the words "Boozefighters MC" painted across its tank.

"No one was going to sit on their bike on the sidewalk and drink that many beers; the cops would run you off," Cameron shook his head and said with the voice of experience. "You *could* do a one-time thing like ride into a bar and then ride out again."

Whatever the truth was, the photo spoke louder than the words of a handful of Boozefighters. Cameron acknowledged the effect it had with a sorrowful shake of his head:

"That photograph changed the image of motorcycling forever. It was one of the most important things that happened to motorcycling in all eternity. That brought on the Hell's Angels and everything

else. They said, 'We'll cash in on this. We'll be the bad guys.' And that started them, and it's a doggone shame."

Watching *The Wild One* these days is like climbing aboard a 1912 Harley-Davidson Silent Gray Fellow and riding off down modern-day streets—you wonder what all the fuss was about. Was this the infernal speed machine that put the fear of God into folk and inspired them to holler "Get a horse"? Movies such as *The Wild Angels*, *The Leather Boys*, *Easy Rider*, and many other biker "classics" today have a period charm. They're timepieces, practically Victorian drawing-room dramas. Hell, they're almost cute.

That's missing the point, however. Watching *The Wild One* in a revival theater from today's vantage point, it's impossible to see the movie and its message from the point of view of the audiences of 1953. Yet the images of fear and loathing that *The Wild One* once inspired toward motorcyclists and their innocent machines were real. After the film opened, you had to be a brave soul to wear a black leather jacket into your local small-town café. Many folk believed that a switchblade was the chief tool you needed to ride a cycle. And it wasn't for naught that when Honda motorcycles were launched in the United States in the early 1960s, the importer spent big bucks on its ad campaign "You Meet the Nicest People on a Honda"; the motorcycle's image needed a haircut, shave, and a new set of respectable clothes.

Today, the town of Hollister holds an annual Independence Day motorcycle race and rally that trades on the commercial value of the 1947 fracas that was once seen as threatening the end of the free world as we know it. Black leather motorcycle jackets are as common as boxer shorts, and if you're a stockbroker or dentist that *doesn't* own a Harley, you stand out from the crowd. *The Wild One*, once the scourge of movie theaters, is a popular video rental. The Hell's Angels even have their own Internet website.

The motorcycle has come full circle in acceptance. The outlaw biker mystique that once shocked and terrified the masses has been subjugated into the mainstream, eaten up by society, and spit out as everyday fashion.

A man went looking for America.
And couldn't find it anywhere...

Cannes Film
Festival
WINNER
"Best Film
By a New
Director"

 easy rider

PANDO COMPANY in association with
RAYBERT PRODUCTIONS presents
starring
PETER FONDA · DENNIS HOPPER · JACK NICHOLSON

Associate Producer   Executive Producer
Produced by   WILLIAM HAYWARD   BERT SCHNEIDER · COLOR
PETER FONDA

Written by   Directed by   Released by COLUMBIA PICTURES
PETER FONDA   DENNIS HOPPER
DENNIS HOPPER    RESTRICTED — Persons under 16
TERRY SOUTHERN   not admitted, unless accompanied
                                         by parent or adult guardian

The Billy Bike:
Re-Born to Be Wild

By David Edwards

As the editor-in-chief of *Cycle World* magazine, David Edwards is one of the primary keepers of the flame for American motorcycling. The magazine he guides covers all aspects of cycling, from the latest and greatest machines to the best vintage classics.

David has a garage filled with an eclectic lineup of machines. From MV Agustas to Indians, he appreciates variety in motorcycles and the history of the species.

This story first appeared in *Cycle World*, profiling one of the milestone motorcycles that has defined Harley-Davidson and cycling pop culture.

Work with me on this. I ask you to name America's most famous motorcycle. You respond with, what, some spindly Nineteen-aughtsomething contrivance from Indian, Excelsior, or Harley-Davidson? Won't cut it, pal—we're talking fame here, celebrity, stature, star power.

Okay, okay, so maybe you nominate something classic from the Steve McQueen collection? Now we're warming up, but you can do better, I know you can. Think mass media.

How 'bout the "Then Came Bronson" Sporty? Evel Knievel's XR-750 busjumper? One of ol' E. A. Presley's Hogs? The Terminator's Fat Boy? Pee-Wee Herman's Hummer? Fuh-get about it!

America's foremost motorsickle is none other than "Captain America," the chrome-framed, flexi-forked, starred-and-striped Harley Panhead chopper ridden by Peter Fonda in that 1969 ode to sex, drugs, and Steppenwolf, *Easy Rider.*

These days it's too easy to dismiss the original *ER* as simply a dopedrenched road picture, *Thelma & Louise* without the T-bird and PMS, but the fact is *Easy Rider* has a high place in Hollywood history. Produced for a paltry $340,000, it has to date grossed more than $50 million. *Time* magazine named it one of the ten most important films of the sixties. It made Jack Nicholson a star and re-ignited the career of Dennis Hopper, never mind that he would quickly extinguish it with near-lethal doses of rum, tequila, and cocaine on a bender that lasted fifteen years.

More germane to our case, *Easy Rider* validated the chopper as a countercultural icon, hell on wheels for the hippie generation. Captain America provided a calling card for young, alienated, rebellious gearheads, and almost overnight everything from Schwinns to CB750s sprouted improbably drawn-out forks and sacrilegious, star-spangled paint schemes.

It also fueled the first cruiser craze. Yep, it would take a few years, but when the suits in the boardrooms realized there was big money to be made, replichops followed—sanitized for your protection, of course. Harley, which previously had pooh-poohed

Easy Rider
Re-release poster for the modern-day western featuring anti-heros Wyatt and Billy on their Harley choppers crafted from ex–Los Angeles Police Department cruisers.

choppers for their biker-gang connections, cuddled right up to the concept and gave us the FX Super Glide. Norton had its HiRider, Kawasaki its KZ900 LTD, Yamaha its XS650 Special. Soon, cruisers would be the best-selling bikes in the country. That's how important Captain America was.

This story is not about that motorcycle.

See, the Captain got top billing, but for those really in the know it was way overdone, too clamorous, a chopper in caricature, all apehangers and fishtail exhausts and sky-high sissybar. No, *Easy Rider's* coolest bike by far was the flamed Panhead ridden by Hopper's character Billy, sort of a spaced-out Kit Carson with a bad haircut.

Hey, don't just take my word for it.

Keith Ball, editor of *Easyriders*, the magazine that takes its name from the movie: "I never liked the Captain America bike; it was too stretched and too gangly-looking. The Billy Bike was more traditional, a 'tighter' custom from a design standpoint."

David Snow, editor of *Iron Horse*, a New York-based hardcore chopper rag: "I wouldn't hesitate to ride either of 'em cross-country, but the Billy Bike is less radical, more sensible than the Fonda bike. As far as riding in the city goes, Billy's bike, with its more compact wheelbase and dragbars, is better suited to splitting lanes and hopping curbs. Captain America would be unwieldy in traffic."

Beau Allen Pacheco, editor of our all-Harley sister book, *Big Twin*: "Watching the movie for the first time, my eyes were riveted on the Captain America bike. But afterwards, the more I thought about it, the Billy Bike is the one I imagined myself riding through the countryside. Captain America looks fragile, like a gazelle. The Billy Bike looks like it was made to ride."

There you have it, I rest my case. The Billy Bike, America's second most famous motorcycle, but first in the hearts of the chopper intelligentsia.

This story is not about that motorcycle, either.

Sad to say, neither machine had an opportunity to bask in its fame. Just prior to the movie's release, they were snagged at gunpoint by scofflaws and sycophants of the first order, unceremoniously broken up for parts, then distributed throughout the chopper underground before their stars ever had a chance to rise.

America's most famous motorcycle
Easy Rider *unwittingly created a countercultural icon—the Harley chopper. After watching the flick at the local movie palace, motorcyclists around the world shut their garage doors and broke out the saws and blowtorches. When the doors opened again, everything from Harleys to Hondas to innocent mini-bikes had been transformed into choppers with impossibly raked forks, "banana" seats, and sissy bars, and had dangerous flames or sacrilegious, star-spangled paint schemes wrapped around them. (Photograph © Brian Blades/Cycle World)*

Graydon Bell Custom

Above: *This is the first custom Graydon Bell ever built. It rides on a Ness Daytec frame with 5 inches (13 cm) of stretch and is powered by Graydon's own 80-ci (1,310-cc) hot-rodded motor. The paint job came from Dave Perewitz with graphics by Nancy Brooks. (Photograph © Timothy Remus)*

Richard Taylor Custom

Right: *Power is the name of the game for Richard Taylor's 120-ci (1,966-cc), twin-supercharged custom. The engine is a Harman push-rod V-twin with Harman cylinder heads and barrels, an S&S crankshaft, Carillo rods, Aries pistons, and Andrews camshafts. The dual KF superchargers feed twin Dell'Orto 45-mm carburetors. Exhuast runs through handmade pipes and mufflers crafted in stainless steel by Taylor. (Photograph © Andrew Morland)*

Glenn Bator has done something to offset that injustice. Bator, 40, is a bike nut with a bike nut's dream job. He oversees the expanding motorcycle collection of media magnate Otis Chandler, in charge of acquisitions, restorations, and general upkeep for Chandler's Vintage Museum in Oxnard, California. So far, the collection numbers about 130, everything from Broughs to Bimotas, Flying Merkels to Munch Mammoths. Eclectic is the key word.

Main thrust, though, is important American motorcycles, which is where *Easy Rider*'s terrible twosome comes in. Three years ago, Chandler commissioned a copy of Fonda's longgone Captain America. Bator, after hundreds of hours spent studying publicity stills, re-running tapes of the movie, and talking to cast and crew members, came up with a deadnuts duplication. Late last year, an exact replica of the Hopper chopper was completed, too, buildtime about nine months.

Research included yet more screenings of the film. "I've watched it over one hundred times now," says Bator, "and when you see it as much as I have, well, it's really a bad movie."

But bleary-eyed diligence paid off in authenticity. Ironically, the originals, which would go on to become cinema's most infamous outlaw bikes (apologies to Brando's *Wild One* Triumph), started life as police motorcycles. Fonda and crew purchased several weary nags at auction after their ticket-dispensing days were done, then tossed the twinshock frames and acquired older Harley "wishbone" rigids, so named because of the kinked shape of the front downtubes.

Bator went the same route with Billy Bike II, rebuilding a 74-inch 1962 FL motor to copspec, namely low-compression pistons and a heavy-duty generator. The 1950s-era frame was treated to red paint but otherwise untouched—unlike Captain America's cage, which had its steering head kicked out to accommodate 12-inch-over fork tubes. The Billy Bike's Wide Glide front end runs a more restrained 6-inch extension, and retains the stock drum brake in lieu of the other bike's stopperless spool hub.

Period accessories abound. The fuel tank is courtesy a Mustang motorbike, heavily reworked, its pearlescent yellow flames applied three times before Bator was finally satisfied they matched the movie bike's. That's a Bates headlight perched ahead of the lower triple-clamp. Fenders front and rear were originally meant to ensconce the wheels of some Britbike or another. Solid handlebar risers and a minimalist sissybar were handfabbed using movie posters and studio 8x10s as a guide. A brass-body Linkert carb wears two signature items: an air cleaner made from a drilled distributor cap and a long, looping throttle cable left dangling in the breeze. Original saddle builder Larry Hooper, retired, was persuaded to replicate his 1968 handiwork, right down to the silver Chevrolet seat studs.

Bator the perfectionist still has a few items to source. A genuine police kickstand for one, a better front fender for another. "Purists may be able to pick a few nits," he says. "It's not quite 100 percent yet, but it's very, very close."

After we took some photographs in the setting sun, it was time to load up both bikes and head for home—with zero break-in miles, the Billy Bike had been trailered to the photo shoot. But Bator couldn't resist the opportunity for a little on-the-road reenactment: "Let's ride 'em back to my house," he enthused. Shotgun-toting rednecks being in (hopefully) short supply around greater Ojai, California, that's just what we did, me playing Hopper, Bator in the Fonda role. Unlike our hapless forerunners, we arrived safely in dusk's last light.

"Well, I guess we just made history," Bator said, smile plastered in place. And we had, too.

Captain America and the Billy Bike, almost thirty years later, together again for the first time.

Re-born to be wild

Overleaf: *For* Easy Rider—*the greatest on-the-road, hippie-biker movie ever made—the motorcycles were built from former Los Angeles Police Department cruisers. Peter Fonda bought four Harley-Davidson Panheads—a 1950, two '51s, and a '52—at an LAPD auction for $500 apiece. These lackeys of the Establishment were about to become the wheels to fuel the anti-Establishment's wildest dream. "I'd designed the extended and mildly raked front forks, helmet, sissy bar, and the tank," Fonda remembered, "but the forty-two degree rake that was suggested by [black activist and sometimes motorcycle customizer] Cliff Vaughs was some piece of work." These recreations follow the originals. Owner: Otis Chandler. (Photograph © Brian Blades/Cycle World)*

Biker Flicks: The Best of the Bad

Biker flicks are genre of their own. They bore names such as *The Wild Angels*, *Hell's Angels Forever*, *Hellriders*, and more with oddly similar titles and plots. These were the movies that our parents warned us about—and with good reason. Their concern had to do with impressionable young minds and the fear that motorcycles would get into our blood. In truth, they should have been more worried about how poorly written, acted, and filmed many of the movies were.

Today, the charm of "classic" biker flicks is that they are so darn bad. As movie critic Leonard Maltin wrote of *The Wild Angels*, it's "OK after about twenty-four beers." And such is their allure.

Angel Unchained

Above: *Now here's a twist! The Hell's Angels team up with the hippies in this 1970 movie to battle the evil rednecks.*

The Wild Angels

Right: *After it was released in 1966, this was considered the biker flick—until Easy Rider changed the name of the game, that is. With stars Peter Fonda, Nancy Sinatra, Bruce Dern, and several assorted Hell's Angels, the cast was loaded with talent.*

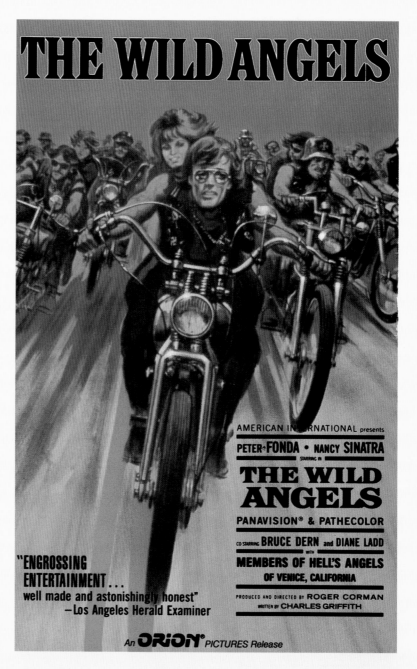

The Wild Rebels

Above: *"They're the Wildest of the Wild Ones!"* promised ads for this 1967 release. With characters named Rod, Fats, Jeeter, Banjo, and Linda, this was classic biker fare.

Hell's Angels '69

Above: *Real, live, breathing Hell's Angels starred in this 1969 gang romp, including Sonny Barger, Tiny, Terry the Tramp, and Magoo. The plot was largely interchangeable with the numerous other Angels flicks: Motorcycles were trashed, chains were swung about, damsels were threatened, etc.*

Born Losers

Left: *This 1967 flick featured a pure Wild-West storyline, with a gang of cycle outlaws terrorizing a small town. Only Tom Laughlin—famous for his later Billy Jack roles—can save the good folks and damsel-in-distress Elizabeth James, who spends her days riding about on a cycle while sporting only an itsy-bitsy bikini.*

The Glory Stompers

Below: *This 1968 flick starred Dennis Hopper and Jody McCrea as leaders of the rival Glory Stompers and Black Souls gangs. As usual, it's another cycle gang war climaxing at the secret nude swimming hole with a combination orgy and rumble.*

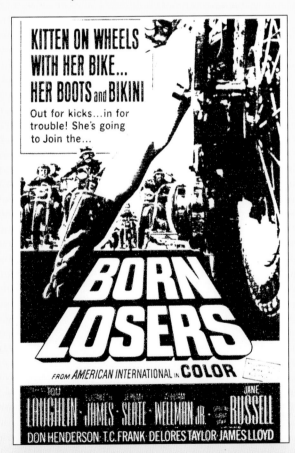

Chapter 6

The Mystique

*"We seemed to breathe more freely,
a lighter air, an air of adventure."*
—Che Guevara, *The Motorcycle Diaries*

Harley-Davidsons are certainly not the only American motorcycles ever built, but to motorcyclists around the world, the Big Twins from the Motor Company are the personification of America. They speak of the United States of myth, a land of endless highways running from sea to shining sea.

Harley-Davidson's mystique is a product of nearly one hundred years of history, during which time its image has been glorified, tarnished, dragged through the mud, and polished once again. Today, the Harley-Davidson mystique is as good as gold, and many people see a Harley as about as all-American as mom and apple pie.

Riding easy
*A blur of motion and the sound of Big Twin power are all that's left when a Harley rides by.
(Photograph © Jerry Irwin)*

V for Victory:
How Harley
Conquered the World

By Ciara Fox

Ever since she bought her first motorcycle at the age of eighteen, Ciara Fox has combed the length and breadth of her native land—Ireland, the land of saints and scholars (though the former are becoming increasingly hard to find)—astride a variety of two-wheeled machines.

Although she endeavored from a young age to lead a devout and chaste life, she failed miserably. Despite being regularly head-hunted by religious institutions, Ciara decided early on to forsake a life of piety for a life of vice. She has lived up to this goal with admirable purposefulness.

Ciara chose to leave the bright lights of the big city behind and headed to western Ireland where she bought a little house in the country, a donkey, a tractor, and some chickens. By day she prostitutes herself to the world of internet development to keep food on the table, but at night she indulges in a nasty journalistic habit, writing for motorcycle publications around the globe.

This essay examines the mystique of Harley-Davidson in Europe.

"Somewhere on a desert highway, She rides a Harley-Davidson, Her long blonde hair flyin' in the wind. . . ."
— Neil Young, "Unknown Legend"

The song just wouldn't have sounded the same if she had been riding a Yamaha or a Ducati. "She rides a Ya-ma-ha-ha-ha. . . ." Nope, it just doesn't cut it. The name *Harley* is as ethereal and flowing as her long, blonde hair as *Davidson* is as definite and determined as the rider herself. Nor would it have worked had she been riding across a German *autobahn*. To those of us in the Old World, there are some essential ingredients that go to mold our view of Americana. Synonymous with the good ole US of A are Cadillac, Route 66, JFK, Coca-Cola, Las Vegas, Neil Young, desert highways, and, of course, Harley-Davidson. All unmistakably American legends, the quintessence of the brave New World. While fashion trends come and go, very often as a result of popular movies and books at any given time, the Harley has withstood passing fads and outlived disposable heroes. Harleys are forever revered in Europe as a

Presidential approval
It doesn't get much more all-American than this. Harley riders round the bend below the approving looks of the presidential visages carved into Mount Rushmore. (Photograph © Jerry Irwin)

unique symbol of the American dream.

Where did the European veneration of Harley-Davidsons come from? When Europe was at the pinnacle of civilization and technological advancement, how did it come to pass that Harleys were created in the New World? Europe had no difficulty in dreaming up some of the most significant milestones in industrial invention such as the camera, the television, and the internal-combustion engine. The possibility of man taking to the skies was an Italian vision way before its time. In a motorcycling context, Frenchman Nicholas Cugnot was propelling tricycles with steam, albeit in a rather cumbersome and fairly unusable manner, as early as 1765. (I suspect that the name of the vehicle was the cause of its downfall—Le Vélocipèdraisavaporianna. Carrying a tank of water to produce the steam was easy compared to trying to pronounce that mouthful!) The boosting of manual pedal power with the aid of auxiliary engines was commonplace in Europe in the 1880s. German Gottlieb Daimler built his first wooden-framed motorcycle with, most significantly, an internal-combustion engine. This heralded a pivotal point in the development of the European motorcycle and indeed influenced the motor industry as a whole.

There were three leading manufacturers of motorcycles in the United States at the dawn of the last century: Indian, Excelsior, and Harley-Davidson. Of these only Harley-Davidson can claim an unbroken lineage. Europe was producing archetypal motorcycles at the beginning of the twentieth century. The British-built Vincent and Brough motorcycles arguably merited the modern-day moniker of "superbike." These record-breaking machines heralded a new era in European motorcycle development. Although the lifeblood of the Brough Superior SS100 of 1928, for example, was carried through a delectable V-twin, 45-bhp, 1000-cc engine—an engine configuration not totally dissimilar to that of the early Harleys—something was changing irrevocably in the evolution of the European motorcycle. As more and more European production bikes began to break the 100-mph barrier, the ever-increasing desire to go faster took precedence. The growing enthusiasm for road racing in the 1910s, such as the Isle of Man TT, resulted in a tunnel vision that led to an obsession with speed. This desire to push the engine and indeed the rider to its limits, although meritorious in itself, spelled the beginning of the myopic journey that European bikes were taking. On the other side of the Atlantic, Harley-Davidson was only finding its feet and determining its direction for the future.

In Milwaukee in 1903, when Messrs. Harley and Davidson entered the engineering arena with an innocuous 2-hp belt-driven machine, little could they have known that the monster V-twins that they were to produce less than ten years later would have such an impact in Europe. Their names would become known to all and sundry, whether interested in motorcycles or not, and Harleys would come to represent something much, much bigger than just a two-wheeled mode of transport. The Harley was a metaphor for freedom and escapism in a society that was sick and tired of going without, of war and depression. But what was it that made Harley-Davidsons stand so far apart from British, German, Italian, and, later, Japanese offerings? What did Harley-Davidson do right, the result of which was the ignition of a passion, veneration, and awe among bikers and non-bikers alike in Europe for Harley-Davidsons?

To make an attempt at answering this question, we must look at the state of the United States and Europe after World War II. The rebuilding of Europe in the postwar years had a huge effect on industry in Europe. No longer allowed to manufacture armaments, many German companies were forced to turn to other lines of production, such as motorcycles. For other European manufacturers, they were compelled to turn their production to arming the war effort. The postwar years was the perfect time to reassess their strategy for the future. New ideas and new technology resulted.

No such restructuring took place in the British bike industry, however. Complacency and over-confidence had set in among British manufacturers. After the war effort, British manufacturers reverted to producing the same leaky and unreliable bikes that they had produced in the past. Engine development stagnated partially due to lack of foreign competition. The major players such as Norton and Triumph ignored the newly introduced scooters that were coming out of Italy. Believing that it was a short-lived fad, they saw no reason to put resources into research

Sunburned cycles

Harleys take in the sunshine on the streets of Daytona Beach, Florida, during the annual Bike Week. (Photograph © Jerry Irwin)

and development of the small runabouts. By the time they realized that scooters were actually big business and here to stay, they were already in dire financial straits. This myopic outlook led to a path of rapid and irreversible decline of sales of British bikes in the late 1960s. Many British bike manufacturers either went out of business altogether, amalgamated with other ailing manufacturers or were forced into buy-outs.

Naturally, foreign competitors were quick to seize the opportunity to enter the British market. The meteoric rise in Japan of motorcycle mass production, spearheaded by Honda, meant that an invasion of Britain was inevitable, prompted by Honda's phenomenal success in the Isle of Man TTs. Here were totally new designs with state-of-the-art technology. In Europe, the race for speed had begun.

At the same time in the United States, Harley-Davidson had mixed a magic and potent formula: large-capacity, torquey engines that were ideal for long and comfortable hauls. These were bikes that took advantage of America's infinite highways. Harley-Davidson produced machines that could eat the miles, effortlessly and efficiently. Thus began a whole new wave of Harley-Davidsons—the big, comfortable, strong, long-distance behemoth. Influenced by the Harleys that had been unwittingly marketed by U.S. servicemen stationed throughout Europe, some Europeans looked west for inspiration, and with Indian long gone, that could only mean a Harley. Harleys were finally making their way into the hearts of Europeans and an enduring love affair had begun.

Owning a stock, shop-bought Harley was an expression of individuality. As unique as Harleys were already, some owners decided that they wanted even more individuality: radically extended forks, an abundance of chrome, lower suspension, elaborate paintwork, and studded leather accessories. As American addicts were bringing their Harleys to an entirely different level, Europeans decided they too wanted a slice of the Harley pie. In an attempt to emulate their American neighbors, Europeans began to spend crazy amounts of money on customizing their Harleys into one-off creations. There were no limitations on what could be done. Shops devoted wholly to customizing Harleys opened up across Europe, such was the demand and the devotion of Harley riders. The Harley-Davidson, the epitome of freedom and strength, had come to Europe in earnest.

The chopped, sit-back-and-relax approach to motorcycling couldn't have hit Europe at a better time. It was the 1960s and just about everyone under forty was sitting back and relaxing—and some of them never got back up again! Although Harley-Davidson had well and truly established itself in Europe in the 1950s, the veneration grew to new heights in the 1960s.

This adoration of Harleys was fueled in no small part by offbeat Hollywood studios that introduced Harley-Davidsons to a wider audience and cemented Harley's place as an icon in the popular canon. Many American B-movies of the 1960s exploited the motorcycle and those who rode them to attract its audiences. These low-budget movies, which for the most part were dire, did absolutely nothing to promote the already deteriorating negative perception of motorcycles among the general population—a perception that had grown with the upsurge in motorcycle gangs. Roger Corman, the undisputed director king of the B-movie, made a phenomenal amount of money for his 1966 movie *The Wild Angels*. This psychedelic experience may be seen as a motorcycle marketeer's nightmare, but to quote the famous Irish wit Oscar Wilde, "There is only one thing worse than being talked about, and that is not being talked about." It also cemented Peter Fonda's idol status among the anti-establishment European youth of the 1960s. Printed images of the Harley he rode in the film sold like hot cakes.

Fonda's 1969 movie *Easy Rider* enjoyed phenomenal success at the box office. Like it or loathe it, *Easy Rider* epitomized the desire to live outside the

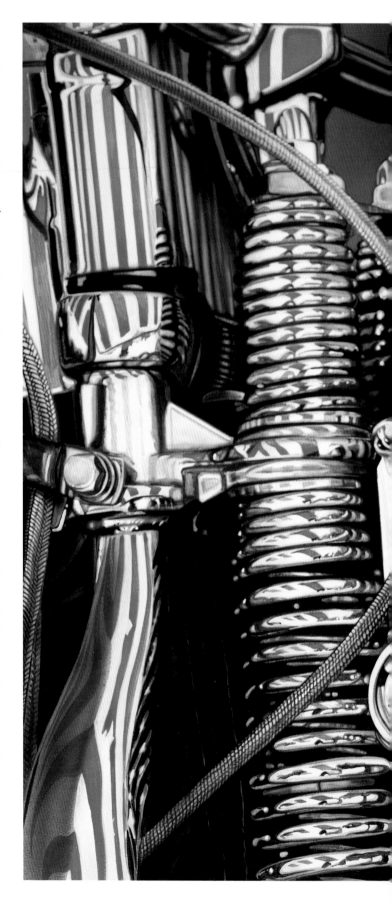

"Stars and stripes"
The American flag reflects off myriad chrome surfaces on the business end of a Harley. James "Kingneon" Guçwa's painting was made with oils on canvas. (Painting © 1999/ Courtesy of Leslie Levy Creative Art Licensing)

rigid constraints of mundane, acceptable society. European audiences lapped it up and contributed considerably to its $60-million profit. Although Fonda claims to have written the film in one night and solely for the purpose of irritating those purists who thought cinema was taking a turn for the worse, the film was nonetheless rich with metaphor for those who wished to take it to a different level. Everything they had was "in that tear-drop gas tank"—the bikes were everything they had. Most people could not help but be mesmerized by the dramatic panoramic shots of Fonda and Hopper riding their Harleys on the open highway. The bikes they rode brought out the best and the worst in the nature of those they encountered on their travels. European audiences fell in love with the Harleys and the freedom and rebelliousness that they symbolized; the transmogrification of man and machine versus the establishment. The movie soon acquired cult status in Europe and had everyone talking about Harleys.

Many later movies featured Harleys. They were a cool, fashionable addition to any movie set. Their very presence added an air of mystique, of sexiness, of rebellion, and often of dissatisfaction to the protagonist. The 1985 film *Mask* was an enormous success with mainstream European moviegoers. A movie about a woman's fight for the rights of her child, Harleys were featured heavily in the film. *Rumble Fish*, an off-the-wall, somewhat self-absorbed, gang violence movie featured a rather sultry Mickey Rourke astride a Harley in several scenes.

Whatever the artistic merit of the movies themselves, *Easy Rider* and *Rumble Fish* in particular both feature some dramatic and unforgettable scenes featuring Harleys. Who can forget the sight in *Easy Rider* of Peter Fonda's Harley being blown apart by a local farmer-gunman as the front end is blasted clean apart from the rest of the bike? Or the scene in *Rumble Fish* where Mickey Rourke revs his bike, jumps off, and lets it fly into a gang member who is beating up on his brother? Some scenes may not have been pleasant but they were effective and memorable. They represented the unity and strength among the Harley fraternity and the constant struggle with non-acceptance. Compared to the European experience of frequently miserable weather, boring roads, and bad bikes, the images portrayed in these movies fueled

the envy of those in Europe. These movies helped to seal the image of Harleys in the public consciousness. While the European moviegoer may have been repulsed by some of the negative imagery in many of these movies, a primordial instinct made the Harley more desirable than ever.

These road movies inspired a whole new industry in Europe—the "Ride-Across-the-U.S.-on-a-Harley" vacation of a lifetime. All of a sudden Europeans wanted to fulfill their dream of crossing the great North American continent on bikes, their trip culminating in California in true clichéd fashion. They wanted to experience the open road. They wanted to pretend to be an "Easy Rider." They wanted to feel tough and cool and invincible. Most of all they wanted to do it on a Harley. They wanted to be able to send postcards to the folks back home boasting that they were cruising on Route 66 on their Electra-Glide, their Fatboy, their Softtail, their Springer, their Sportster, or their Low Rider. It may have been full of clichés but it sounded sexy and they felt sexy. To those in Europe, America had to be crossed on a Harley or not at all.

Many prudent European business-minded bikers and tour operators saw this as a viable business opportunity. Forget the packaged fun-in-the-sun vacation or the exorbitantly-priced luxury cruise. Tour operators now package motorcycling holidays around the world. In Africa, your bike of choice may be a big trail bike and in Europe it may be a Gold Wing. But in the United States it just has to be a Harley. There doesn't seem to be any point in doing it on any other bike. Ultimately, the trip is not only about seeing what lies in between the East and the West coasts. It's the whole experience, the romance, the mystery. It's not about how fast you go. It's the challenge of doing it. It's being able to say you did it. It's about how to look cool, and it doesn't get much cooler than on a Harley. The European dream of being that Easy Rider can finally become a reality.

Harley-Davidsons have penetrated other aspects of society in Europe. So widespread has the epidemic of Harley fever been in Europe, that Harleys have been elevated to a new level by the general public. Harley apparel, appurtenances, and paraphernalia have become a symbol of affluence and classiness, while paradoxically representing rebelliousness at the same time. Across Europe in the 1990s, it became possible for those who couldn't ride a Harley and who indeed had no intention of ever riding a Harley to become part of the club. They wore the jackets, the jeans, the t-shirts, the bandanas, they held the jeans up with Harley belts, they lit their Gitanes with their Harley lighters, and they strutted their stuff in their cool Harley-Davidson boots. The people were a world away from those Harley aficionados who actually rode the bikes and to a large extent the two camps were on opposing sides of the fence. Today, the catwalks of Milan and Paris are no longer the preserve of the Versaces and Ralph Laurens of this world; super-models now sport Harley-Davidson clothing at the most publicized fashion shows in Europe. The Harley has been brought into the popular consciousness and pop culture, and this icon of perceived rebellious-ness and easy-living has become, ironically, an icon

Main street

Sturgis, South Dakota, glows at night in the neon glare of main street's lights and the headlamps from a thousand Harleys. (Photograph © Jerry Irwin)

1941 Harley-Davidson WLDR
The 1941 WLDR was a true racer sold by the Motor Company equipped with full road gear. Unlike many WLDRs, which were stripped down for racing, this cycle bears many road accessories and upgrades that were available at extra charge from the factory. Owner: Armando Magri. (Photograph © Nick Cedar)

of respectability.

As if Harley clothing wasn't enough, Europeans want to eat Harley! Harley cafés and restaurants are popping up in the capitals and major cities of Europe. More significantly, these eateries aren't relegated to seedy, off-the-tourist-trail backstreets. They are located in the most affluent parts of town. The interiors are adorned with all manner of Harley-Davidson iconography: autographed pin-up photographs of movie and rock stars and their Harleys, American flags, and, of course, posters from *Easy Rider*. Most of these establishments possess an actual living Harley-Davidson, suspended from the ceiling or poised on a platform behind a barrier and guarded by burly security people. Apart from being a great source of advertising for Harley-Davidson, the existence of these restaurants and cafés has been another notch in the Harley belt. They provide the link between the biker and the non-biker. They have be-

come an intrinsic part of European mainstream society—the ultimate commodity of unashamed decadence and status for both the frustrated rebel in search of a cause and also the ideal of unparalleled freedom for the tired, railroaded ordinary citizen.

So that's where Harley-Davidson stands in Europe today. An inherent part of European life, a slice of Americana that Europeans dream about.

Harley-Davidsons also provide a historic link to the past. Harleys have been around in some form or another since 1903. That's almost a hundred years of continuous motorcycle production. The essence of the big, thumping V-twin has remained largely unchanged since the 1930s. The timeless, traditional style has endured for over seventy years. Harleys contrast totally with the disposable, cloned, plastic bikes of other manufacturers whose models are outdated as soon as they hit the road, manufacturers whose only concern is outspeeding the competition. At the end of the day, all they are producing are forgettable machines with empty promises. The whole *raison d'être* of motorcycling has been utterly lost.

Harley-Davidson has not forgotten what motorcycling is all about. The company does not need to obsess with competing with other manufacturers as there is no real competition. Other manufacturers produce the occasional token copycat bike in a vain attempt to cash in on the Harley-Davidson mystique, but no matter how highly engineered they make the copycats, no matter how many bells and whistles they put on them, Harleys remain in a league of their own. The company has been able to build on almost a century of experience, creating classic machines and nurturing a rapport with Harley riders. Harley knows its bikes and, perhaps more importantly, it knows its customers and what they want. Harley-Davidson has spent nearly a hundred years improving the breed rather than trying to create a totally new species simply for the sake of profit. No other bike manufacturer can make similar claims. To quote from the latest Harley-Davidson European catalog for 2000: "Who cares what millennium it is?" Harley-Davidsons are timeless. Riding a Harley is about seeing things in a totally different way. This is life as it is meant to be.

As for me, a few years ago I would never have considered myself a Harley rider. I knew that being a Harley rider was a vocation and I had not received the calling. I knew Harleys were not for everyone, that they were reserved for the chosen few. Harleys riders were a breed apart, untouch-able and remote. My interests lay in having the latest techno-wonder. My days were spent riding with hormonally fueled people whose only aim was to outdo each other. There was little sense of camaraderie, no sense of brother- and sisterhood. My riding was a headlong plunge into the depths of rivalry. There was no time to enjoy the world around me. With hindsight I realize that this wasn't me or for me. I have begun to appreciate the finer things in life. I have pulled back from the stressful, over-legislated, homogenized rat race that constitutes most Europeans' conformist lives. I am ready to make the transition from simply riding bikes to being a Harley rider.

I hope this year that somewhere on a motorway, I'll be riding a Harley-Davidson with my long brown hair flyin' in the wind. . . .

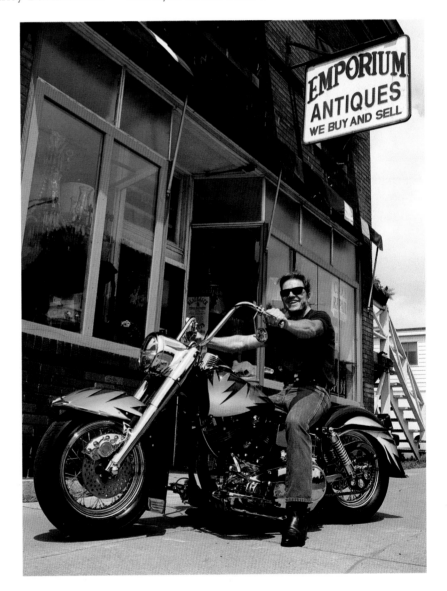

Tom Fedorowski Custom
This custom started life as your straight-ahead 1979 Harley-Davidson FLH. The paint was shot by master Mallard Teal. Owner: Tom Fedorowski. (Photograph © Andrew Morland)

This Motorcycle Way

By Dr. Martin Jack Rosenblum

Dr. Martin Jack Rosenblum is the Historian for the Harley-Davidson Motor Company.

Among Martin's numerous published and recorded works are *The Holy Ranger: Harley-Davidson Poems* (a Harley-Davidson licensed product) and *The Holy Ranger's Free Hand* (Rounder Records).

Martin composes on a 1901 Underwood No. 5 typewriter, which is nearly as loud as a Harley-Davidson motorcycle should be. Computers are too quiet for him and frighten his desire for mystical delight.

I.

I was initially attracted to Harley-Davidson motorcycles because of the sound they made. I lived in a rural town and often heard motorcycles blasting along the dirt and gravel roads near my house, and the Harley's exhaust note was rather like the blues compared to teen-idol music. I would try to match that sound on my Schwinn bicycle by putting playing cards on the rear fender braces with clothespins to hold them in place while they rubbed against the spokes, producing what I felt could be the sound of a Harley-Davidson.

I would try to catch the motorcyclists as they went by my house, heading for someplace that certainly was, no doubt, mysterious and secret. The local policemen would also try to catch these bikeriders and one morning I came upon an Appleton, Wisconsin, police officer on a Harley Servi-Car, hiding in the brush along the Fox River hill road.

The bikeriders would race along this road until it came up near my house and would throttle hard, coming off the stones onto blacktop. I probably saved one of these motorcyclists that morning because I asked the policeman for a ride, and he consented, letting me sit on the box while he drove around my neighborhood.

My Schwinn suddenly was no longer the two-wheeled vehicle with which I identified. I had to have a motorcycle, a Harley-Davidson.

I hung out with the older guys who rode motorcycles, and they would often permit me to drive over fields and on back roads. We listened to Gene Vincent back at their clubhouse, and one of these bikeriders even had a Gibson archtop guitar, left at his house by an uncle who was a hillbilly singer in place of the rent he owed my friend's parents, and he could struggle through a raw version of "Dance To The Bop."

And sometimes Anne would actually dance the bop, right there on the rutted lawn, blond hair rolling with her shoulders as she twirled her black scarf around in the air, stepping in saddle shoes to the broken beat coming from the Gibson.

I would often go over to Anne's house, too, as

"The King and I"
Neon lights create a halo around the latest Harley-Davidson Road King in James "Kingneon" Guçwa's acrylics-on-canvas painting. (Painting © 1999/Courtesy of Leslie Levy Creative Art Licensing)

she lived just down the street; and one time she was in the shower when I walked in. The door was always open in those days. I knew she could tell I was in the living room of her house, because she started to hum just a little the way you do when you know someone is listening. My damn Schwinn was leaning out front, next to the broken porch railing, and I wished I could have a Harley out there instead, and that Anne was getting all cleaned up for me and we would ride.

As I looked out of the stained window, one of the Harley riders from the club, the one that I thought was her boyfriend, pulled up; he would not mind that I was there. I was no threat. I was just a kid. So I turned to tell Anne I heard Dwight pull up and there she was, nothing but a towel wrapped around her, wet but with red lipstick already on, and smiling at me the way an older sister would if she was wondering about what a little brother might really be.

Dwight killed his bike, and I heard the sidestand go down. Anne asked me if she looked pretty for Dwight. I said she looked just fine. Dwight came in and they kissed and then Anne disappeared to get dressed, and Dwight looked at me and said, "Jack, you can't come along tonight."

II.

When I finally was old enough to get my own Harley, my father, a Swedish immigrant, had other ideas about my preference, saying that motorcycles, especially a Harley, were too loud for the calm and staid American front lawn he had worked so hard to achieve. He suggested another bicycle, even one with more chrome, perhaps, which I could then also use on my paper route.

I chose to walk the route and hide the Harley in my grandma's chicken coop. Grandma liked to spoil me. She lived just through the ravine, so after delivering all the papers, I would get my Harley-Davidson and ride it as far as I could and still be home for supper.

III.

That motorcycle defined who I was, even though I

had to hide it. Actually, I had to hide who I was anyway. I was raised in an orthodox Jewish home and when wearing my black engineer boots, bluejeans rolled up over them, and my thick, black belt with the brass buckle on the side and motorcycle cap, I was unknown. The rabbi lectured me. My mother looked at my ducktail haircut as though I wore it to make her angry. At school, I was supposed to be popular, but hung out with Dwight and his buddies so my social friends often held me in great disdain. At sporting events I sat with the bikeriders, and even got drunk once and fell out of the stands right on top of a cheerleader who was tying her tennis shoes. When she glared at me I wanted to say, "Hey, babe, I saw Anne in red lipstick, still wet from bathing, wearing just a towel, so don't get all upset." But instead I apologized and felt stupid.

I never felt dumb when I throttled-up on my Harley, dancing on late night pavement, screaming over the back roads traveled only by miscreants and prophets. I grew up in this motorcycle way. I knew who I was when I rode.

IV.

School was of no interest until I went from Rockabilly to Cool Jazz, and became a beatnik. Suddenly, it was all right to be smart. I even got a Triumph motorcycle, forsaking my Harley because it was too greasy. I published my first book of poems. I had learned how to play guitar on an old Stella that my father

Mallard Teal Custom
Paint maestro Mallard Teal crafted this Harley-Davidson "café racer" riding atop an SBF frame. The 93-ci (1,523-cc) engine provides the muscle. (Photograph © Andrew Morland)

Yes, Virginia, there really is a Santa Claus . . .
Left: *. . . and he rides a Harley. Natch. (Photograph © Jerry Irwin)*

took in trade when one of his customers could not pay the bill. Guitars fell into our hands then, it seemed, as though parts of a tab, never to be shopped for and bought out front. I could handle some songs but it was not until the end of my beatnik days that I became proficient on guitar. I signed up for the Folk/ Blues Revival, as it later was known, and actually shopped for my first Gibson. I got a J-50. My Dad took a day off of work to drive me to Milwaukee to buy it. That was the first day he ever took off, and the last, although he did not think that playing folk music, certainly not writing poetry, was anything but a better hobby than riding motorcycles.

But it was motorcycling that somehow guided these interests. By this time there were people called bikers, and I was one of them. The extent to which I could descend into the Blues came from the ride, and the meter of my poetic line to which I ascended roared out of the engine pulse. I was back on a Harley-Davidson motorcycle, as I did not sing any of those English ballads. I stomped traditional American blues music.

I was soon in college, doing quite well. My study of American literature, history, and culture resulted in three degrees, over twenty-five books and a half-dozen recorded albums and, before becoming the Historian for the Harley-Davidson Motor Company, nearly a quarter century in academia as a teacher and student advisor. I rode a Harley. It all made sense because this American motorcycle tied it together in ways I shall never comprehend. William Carlos Williams in his book, *In The American Grain*, says that "I speak of aesthetic satisfaction. This want, in America, can only be filled by knowledge, a poetic knowledge." I am satisfied to demand no more than poetic knowledge of this motorcycle way, even though I spend countless scholastic hours in pursuit of its history on American soil. The roots of it, though, are so deep that:

When a Harley-Davidson motorcycle
Comes out of the turn and the engine sound
Rattles gutter leaves and even windows in my home
There is an aesthetic from the smell of it and the scramble
To see it though you have seen thousands like it but not this one.

Seasoned cyclist
Above: *Watching the Harleys go by on main street in Sturgis, South Dakota. (Photograph © Jerry Irwin)*

"Backroads"
Facing page: *Artist Kent Bash created this oil-on-canvas image of a Harley on a blue highway. (Painting © Kent Bash)*

V.

No one will ever understand any of this, and no one should. It cannot possibly be explained. But it may be poetically known. It all has to do with the way by which history and culture collide, creating personal lore that is at once legitimate fact and real legend. This way of the motorcycle by which we know our own souls better and in ways mythopoetic assign soulful attributes to our Harley-Davidsons is shamanistic. But I prefer just to consider on most nights, usually right after I park my Springer Softail in the garage and the light has clicked off by itself once the door has shut, to remember what Dwight once said to me as we sat out in front of Anne's house. He said, "Man, look at my bike. Martin Jack, look at my bike. You got to have one of your own. No telling where it will take you, man, no telling."

Gathering of the clan

A Harley lover's dream come true: main street in Sturgis, South Dakota, during the annual summer gathering of the clan. (Photograph © Andrew Morland)

Harley-Davidson Road King

This Road King was given a well-deserved Midas touch with gold plating to highlight its engine. Owner: Gilles Sauvageau and Yvan Jodoin. (Photograph © Andrew Morland)

"The Great American Freedom Machine."
—Harley-Davidson slogan, 1970s

1936 Harley-Davidson 61 OHV Model EL
The arrival of Harley-Davidson's overhead-valve Big Twin inspired ecstasy among dealers—one of whom saw fit to unleash a fusillade of bullets from his six-gun into the air at the unveiling in pure, unadulterated glee. Such contagious celebration seems fitting in hindsight as the Knucklehead became the secret weapon that won the war with Indian—and evolved into the engine that powers Harleys to this day. Owner: Carman Brown. (Photograph © John Dean/Reynolds-Alberta Museum)

The King's Harley

This story has just got to be true—at least all Harley enthusiasts would like to believe in it.

Elvis Presley was a big fan of Harley-Davidsons. As soon as his first records went gold, he bought a Harley, which he rode on as if it were a throne. He continued to order almost annually the latest and greatest from Milwaukee. And the King never skimped on accessories, either.

Alas, this tale is as tall as they come. It's a classic bike-in-the-barn yarn that's been repeated so many times far and wide that it has become a modern urban legend.

Public relations people at Harley merely laugh at the story because they've heard it so many times. Besides, the Motor Company already owns one of the King's pride and joys, a 1956 Harley-Davidson Model KH that is proudly displayed in the firm's York, Pennsylvania, museum. The Graceland Museum in Memphis, Tennessee, already has five of Elvis's machines—four Harleys and one Honda. And Jay Leno has even posted an official denial on *The Tonight Show*'s website so people will stop asking him about the story.

I was chatting with a Harley-riding friend the other day when he told me a tale that made the valves over-rev in my heart. He promised that the story was true. A friend of his knew the person it happened to.

This was his story:

"A friend of a friend of a friend's friend of mine was out riding his Harley-Davidson down a country road on a beautiful summer day with nothing but Harleys on his mind. He rode past grazing Holstein cows that appeared to him like raw material to re-upholster his FLSTN Heritage Softtail Nostalgia 'Moo-Glide.' He saw a classic red barn and filed the color away in his mind to match when painting his Model 61 OHV Knucklehead restoration project.

"Suddenly, he spotted a sight along the side the road that diverted his train of thought. There stood an old, decrepit Harley-Davidson parked in front of a farm with a hand-lettered 'For Sale' sign hanging from the handlebars. He hit the brakes and jumped off to take a gander. Under the years of grime, road dirt, and some stray pieces of straw, it looked like a complete mid-1950s Harley and did not even appear to have many miles on it. Then warning signals started going off in his brain like a backfiring Shovelhead: The owner probably wants a bundle for it.

"Soon said owner came ambling out from the farmhouse with a corncob pipe dangling from his mouth. He was your stereotypical farmer: Straw hat, work boots, faded denim overalls, red bandanna hanging from his back pocket—the traditional American folk costume.

"'Y'all have an interest in this little ol' cycle?' he asked.

"'Maybe,' my friend of a friend of a friend's friend replied, hedging his interest behind noncommittance in the time-honored motorcycle collector's manner.

"He casually walked another lap around the bike, shaking his head and grimacing at its condition while inside his heartbeat accelerated like an XR-750 down a straightaway.

"'What's the story?' he asked in his best bored tone.

"'Weeellll,' the farmer started like he had all day to tell the tale, 'a friend of a friend of my son's friend found this here cycle somewheres, but his pa wouldn't let him keep it. So, he sold it to the friend of my son's friend, but he rode it once and it was just too big a hoss for him. So, he sold it to my son's friend, but he broke a joint or something in the engine. So, he gave it to my son, who parked it in the barn there about ten years ago and plum forgot about it. So, the other day, I was mucking out the barn and dragged the cycle out of a pile of hay, wheeled out to the rode here, hung that 'For Sale' sign on it, and then you showed up.'

"'So, uh, how much do you want for it?' he asked, making certain not to look at the farmer.

"The farmer didn't make eye contact either when he named his price, 'Oh, about $400.'

"My friend of a friend of a friend's friend's heart began skipping beats like an Evolution engine with its timing off.

"'Well, OK. That seems fair,' he said a bit too quickly.

"The deal was done. My friend of a friend of a friend's friend revved his Harley up, sped home, and returned that afternoon to haul away the motorcycle.

"When he got the bike into his workshop, he made a list of parts he would need to get the machine back on the road. He called his neighborhood Harley dealer, but they didn't carry parts for a model that old. So he dialed up the grand old Motor Company itself in Milwaukee, speaking in a hushed, reverent tone to describe the Harley and request parts.

"The person he spoke to in the parts department, asked him to describe the bike again, then put him on hold. Another person came on the line, asked for the description, then transferred the call. Soon, my friend of a friend of a friend's friend was transferred through a dozen people, each wanting to hear the cycle's description before passing him on to a higher level. Finally, the CEO himself of the whole Harley kingdom came on the line and asked to hear the story.

"'Can you please describe the cycle one more time,' the CEO pleaded with him. Then he told my friend of a friend of a friend's friend to check under the rear fender of the cycle and report if he found anything special.

"And there, under that rear fender, were inscribed the words, 'To Elvis . . .'

"Needless to say, my friend of a friend of a friend's friend's breath caught in his throat like a WR with too constrictive of a carburetor venturi.

"He reported his finding to the Motor Company CEO, who told him the tale: 'That's Elvis's long-lost Harley-Davidson. It was a gift to him from James Dean, specially

Elvis

The King sat astride a Harley-Davidson Big Twin like he was perched on his throne. As soon as Elvis Presley's first records went gold, he bought a Harley—and continued to order almost annually the latest and greatest from Milwaukee. The King never skimped on accessories, either.

inscribed under that fender. I'll give you $2 million for it right now.'"

We sat in silence for a moment and let the story kick in. I shook my head.

"So what happened?"

"Well," my friend said, "this friend of a friend of a friend's friend of mine knew he had something hot. So he told the CEO of all of Harley-Davidson that he'd have to think on it. He'd call him back.

"But the story got out somehow, and the next day he got a call from no less than Lisa Marie Presley herself at Graceland wanting to hear about the missing motorcycle of her father's and offering him $3 million!

"He told Lisa Marie he'd think on it, and no sooner had he hung up than Jay Leno himself called from set of *The Tonight Show* and offered $4 million."

"And so what did he do?" I asked.

"Oh, he's still got the bike and he's still getting offers on it," my friend said. "Who knows where it'll all end."

"Gosh," I said, "I don't have the money to make an offer, but I'd sure like to just see the King's Harley. Can we ride over and look at it?"

"*Weeellll,*" my friend said, just like the farmer in the story, "I don't actually *know* the guy. See, he's a *friend* of a friend of a friend of a friend's friend."

The Perfect Vehicle

By Melissa Holbrook Pierson

Melissa Holbrook Pierson's 1997 book *The Perfect Vehicle: What it is About Motorcycles* is a road-trip travelogue, philosophical treatise, and love story all rolled into one. The object of all this affection is naturally enough the motorcycle.

This is not *Zen and the Art of Motorcycle Maintenance*, however. Pierson summons forth ghosts of motorcycling days past, colorful historical anecdotes, myth and hyperbole, two-wheeled pop culture, and tales of women enthusiasts. All of this is intermixed with Pierson's own story, her roaming across the United States, and her love affair with a certain perfect machine.

 From my mother I learned to write prompt thank-you notes for a variety of occasions; from Mrs. King's ballroom dancing school I learned a proper curtsy and, believe it or not, what to do if presented with nine eating utensils at the same place setting, presumably at the home of the hosts to whom I had just curtsied. From motorcycles I learned practically everything else.

In the ten years that I've been on and around them, motorcycles have given me plenty of metaphoric chalk talks. There has been a lot about the nature of the arbitrary, the grace of sudden change. The illustrations are curious. One day, say, you can be in graduate school, sweating over blazingly irrelevant papers on *Sir Gawain and the Green Knight* and yet another reading of Hawthorne, looking forward to a life behind library stacks and lecterns while wearing muted silk scarves and subtle glasses. And the next you can be out of there so entirely you have grease beneath your fingernails as you bump-start your bike down a hill after a fuse blew, or you wake up extra early on Sunday morning to make the seventy miles to the parking lot of a diner in Danbury, Connecticut, just to gaze upon the sight of a couple hundred bikes that are there because of the same impulse. Or perhaps none of this is so strange after all and I am merely fulfilling the appraisal of William F. Buckley, Jr., who called all of us in my college class "ferocious illiterates" after we disinvited him from giving our graduation address in 1980.

A motorcycle becomes an extension of yourself, your body and faculties and hopes and pathologies—and I learned that mine could give me the sort of information it is painful to receive, which is how you know (according to psychologists) it is true. In holding out the need to maintain and repair it, my motorcycle would quickly transform itself into a mirror at the moment I raised the wrench toward it, so that I was really turning bolts inside myself, the ones that confusingly wished to come cleanly out and at the same time were stuck fast, apparently waiting for someone better than me to rescue them from myself. I also appreciated the teachings of the other bolts, such as the ones holding the brake rotors to the front wheel, which wouldn't budge no matter how hard I whaled on them or with what, just as I was especially grateful for the ones under the valve covers that I

1959 Harley-Davidson FLH Duo-Glide
It was the ride of choice for Elvis Presley. It defined American motorcycles. It was Harley-Davidson's flagship model in 1959, and things just couldn't get any better. (Photograph © Andrew Morland)

learned to adjust perfectly, taking small increments and making them smaller in order to reach the point of equilibrium when the feeler gauge under the tappets is held just snugly enough, a point attained by sensation and nothing else. That is true satisfaction.

There were some interesting global lessons, too, like the simple but easily overlooked fact that alone of animals we are primarily marked by our passions. For some it's the Grateful Dead; for others Gilbert and Sullivan. Partisans of old Airstreams follow other Airstream lovers across the country to meet at rallies and celebrate the object of their affection as well as the fact that they found one another. Then there is the inexplicable obsession shared only by train spotters, for whom no explanation is needed. Some Americans seem to have no hobby at all, you say? Certainly they do, if the definition of a hobby is something that takes up all your time, love, and extra cash: that would be children. And then there are motorcycles, which are just like children to some of their owners, the hard core.

I am not referring to outlaw bikers. A small minority of all riders, the highly visible, self-proclaimed one-percenters (as they consider their numbers in relation to those of the less colorful majority), have perhaps understandably taken the spotlight. Still, if I see yet another glossy photo essay on tattooed hellions accompanied by earnest text explaining to a horrified but titillated Middle America that their bikes are called "hogs," I think I'll scream.

Of course, there are "gangs" (they call themselves clubs, as do most clubs that are in no way gangs). If you're wearing the patch, or colors, of your club on the back of your jacket as you ride through the territory claimed by, say, the Pagans, they will request that you furl your flag. The Hell's Angels still exist, too, although they remain a very small fraction of all motorcyclists and have perhaps graduated from the quaint type of brutal mischief catalogued in Hunter S. Thompson's 1966 *Hell's Angels*. They are today, according to a news item quoting international police intelligence sources, a "world crime threat" and "as likely to drive a BMW series 7 as a motorcycle." As for the public fixation on these lively few, I am finding it increasingly tedious, as if the night only consisted of one moonrise and not a billion stars too. It is perhaps understandable, given our desire to see

humans as capable of anything; either extreme of behavior or achievement will apparently do the trick. If we actually looked at the vast interior cordoned off by these two points, however, we would find ourselves. Anything as unexamined as the normal heart has got to have a few interesting things to be said about it.

Another of those aha lessons concerned group allegiance, that which leads warriors to die behind the banner of their nation. It is present in even the smallest domains, as any partisan of competitive sports well knows. In order to determine one's group affiliation, however, one has to define the group. People with brown skin and straight hair? People who believe that if they strap on a suicide bomb and enter a public square filled with heathens they will become heroes in heaven? Thus among some bikers there is an argument going on that ranges from barely voiced to openly acrimonious: What is a "real" biker? Contrary to expectation, it does not date to the recent fashionableness of motorcycles (primarily Harleys) among people who in previous decades might have incredulously denied the possibility that they would ever look twice at a motorcycle, much less with longing. These people are called RUBs (rich urban bikers), in part because these days one must have a zippy acronym for everything. Long before the age of the RUBs, however, bikers were delimiting themselves. A few have always refused to get entangled, professing a noble egalitarianism: anyone who likes bikes is a biker. But the main grist of letters columns in bike magazines the world over is the exchange of accusations that one type or another of biker, being untrue, is ruining the reputation of the sport. . . .

The hardcore lover of motorcycles, the one whose head turns at every growing sound that promises a bike will soon flash into view, can't help it. There is a peculiar kind of motolust that inspires some people to fill their garages with bikes and the "pre-restored" carcasses thereof and still be unable to resist the next one they see that has a for-sale sign around its neck. They go away for a weekend of riding and come back with new friends whom they stay up with half the night talking of bikes and other destinations at which they will meet new people who will phone them the following week to tell of further destinations. The

Perfect vehicles
Miniature motorcycles provided inspiration, education, and hours of fun for children—of all ages—around the world. Memorabilia owner: Doug Leikala. (Photograph © Nick Cedar)

"The Buddha, the Godhead, resides quite as comfortably om the circuits of a digital computer or the gears of a cycle transmission as he does at the top of a mountain or in the petals of a flower."
—Robert M. Pirsig, *Zen and the Art of Motorcycle Maintenance*, 1974

calendar fills; the season is not long enough. The pocketbook is rarely large enough, for bikes, like boats, are black holes in the universe of money.

Riding on a motorcycle can make you feel joyous, powerful, peaceful, frightened, vulnerable, and back out to happy again, perhaps in the same ten miles. It is life compressed, its own answer to the question "Why?"

Why? they ask, those who don't ride. Those who do ride are incapable of understanding the question. Riding feels good, they say—it feels damn good. But I think there is more, just as there is always more underneath the obvious, and a little more underneath that. The great layered mysteries of human motivation are oddly both variegated and amazingly uniform. And they are revealed in the many reasons, as well as the one simple one, why people ride.

Motorcycles are what they feel like (profoundly sensual—vroom, vroom—and perhaps a bit primordial) and also what they look like (fearsome, with a strange deep beauty). Look at that engine, out for anyone to see, and those two simple wheels: what else announces its intent so brazenly? It is not simply a coincidence that after World War II some ill-fitting veterans came home to ride these particular machines in angry bunches, giving birth to the myth and reality of gangs like the Hell's Angels. Just as it was not insignificant that T. E. Lawrence bought the farm, riding back from the post office at a very reasonable rate of speed, on one of his beloved Brough Superiors.

Colin Wilson counted Lawrence among the exemplary "outsiders" in his book of the same name, and he explained the adventurer's central motive: "His clear-sighted intellect could not conceive of moral freedom without physical freedom too; pain was an invaluable instrument in experiments to determine the extent of his moral freedom." Motorcyclists intuitively understand this even if they cannot articulate it, just as they would identify with Lawrence's penchant for riding his lovely machine, which he named Boanerges, flat-out for speed, and sometimes to race a fighter plane flying overhead. "A skittish motor-bike with a touch of blood in it is better than all the riding animals on earth, because of its logical extension of our faculties, and the hint, the provocation, to excess conferred by its honeyed

1959 Harley-Davidson FLH Duo-Glide

Above: *The Motor Company had finally—almost regrettably—won out in its nearly six-decades-long Big Twin war with Indian, and was sitting pretty as the ultimate two-wheeled dream machine. The overhead-valve, 45-degree Panhead V-twin displaced 74 cubic inches (1,212 cc) and was rated at 60 bhp. The swing-arm rear suspension and hydraulic telescopic forks defined the Duo-Glide moniker. This FLH was the state of the art in 1959. Owner: Martin Gale. (Photograph © Andrew Morland)*

"Let the Good Times Roll"

Overleaf: *Dave Barnhouse's oil painting captures the spirit of the ride. (the Hadley Companies)*

untired smoothness," he wrote. "Because Boa loves me, he gives me five more miles of speed than a stranger would get from him."

Motorcyclists understand this too, because what bikes feel like is an extension of the self—a better you, a perfectible, fixable you, an ominously powerful you. That is also what they look like to the occasionally cowed bystander, who, like an Indian first seeing a white man on horseback, may believe he has encountered some new creature that is only part human.

To those who love motorcycles deeply, there is usually one aspect of the machine that broadcasts its allure in advance of all others. It may be the visual arrangement of parts, their rake and line and organization that come together in a design that seems to freeze speed. It may be the look of meanness, sweetness, or promise delivered even from under the fluorescent light of the showroom. For me, it is their sound that makes the heart race. The exhaust note of certain bikes functions like an aria, the relentlessly plaintive song that arrives at the vulnerable moment in the opera to wring the emotions dry.

Every model has its characteristic melody, and maybe if you love your bike you simply love its sound most. (Harley-Davidson is now attempting to trademark the sound of its engine against pretenders who would seek to duplicate the tune of a 45-degree V-twin with a single crank pin.) The sounds of Italian engines, especially those of Moto Guzzis and Ducatis, are to me so supremely sensuous that I can only merely appreciate—albeit appreciate well—the tone of other bikes. And believe me, I am not alone: the Swedish Ducati Club has produced a CD titled *Ducati Passions*, a recording of a dozen different models of the renowned machines from Bologna, from a 1958 55/e to a 1993 M900 Monster, as they move up and down the gears; the liner notes include information on each bike's exhaust system and warn overenthusiastic listeners to take it easy with the volume so as not to blow their speakers.

My friend Erica, who when we were children loved horses with a passion that has only been equaled by what she now feels for bikes, owns a Moto Guzzi and a Ducati. She is known to swoon at the sound of their kin on the street or track, but she is not tone-deaf to the other great songs of the motorcycle

world, either. As a vintage British BSA Gold Star went by, her eyes grew larger and larger and she exclaimed with childlike amazement, "It's like the heavens have opened up!" A British writer—the Brits are especially finely attuned to the poetry of the man-made world—described the sound of a Yamaha enduro model as "a shopful of timpani getting showered with marbles."

I would know the sound of a big Guzzi in my sleep. It concentrates its aural energies in your upper chest, ringing through your bones. It's not the fat blatting of a Harley—the heavy metal of exhaust music—often released at unbelievable levels by aftermarket pipes, nor is it the sheer scream of a high-revving Japanese crotch rocket. It is, rather, the sound of joy, as is, say, the bass tune of a Ducati 851 roaring inches away down the straightaway of a racetrack at well over 100 mph. The sight is a flash of red, impossible to see except as a blur at close range, but the swelling, deepening waves of sound as it retreats stay with you, pinning you solidly to the ground through your feet.

In the quite dignified old suburb of Akron, Ohio, where I grew up, the warm months were full of soft sibilance: crickets rasping, moths hitting screen, the

1995 Buell Thunderbolt S2T
Facing page, top: Erik Buell's Thunderbolt tourer represented a true twist to both Buell and Harley history. Buell originally stepped away from the Motor Company to build his own sporting machines. Once his S1 Lightning and S2 Thunderbolt established themselves, he returned to his roots as it were and offered a sports tourer in the form of the 1995 S2T. As Buell's flagship model, it nicely bridged the gap between Buell "sportsters" and Harley full dressers. (Photograph © Andrew Morland)

1992 Harley-Davidson Softail Springer
Facing page, bottom: In 1988, the Motor Company took a giant step back in time. Way back when the first Harley-Davidsons were built, engineer and founding father William S. Harley created a front fork design with leading-link suspension that was so good that it lasted for almost five decades and was blatantly copied far and wide. Now, retro was in, and the Springer was introduced with leading-link suspension and the springs mounted boldly out in front where everyone had to notice them. The nostalgia boom of the 1990s saluted the Springer with strong sales. William S. Harley could be proud. Owner: Ronald Torbich. (Photograph © Andrew Morland)

1964 Harley-Davidson XLH Sportster

The first Sportster was not just a rehabilitated Model KH fitted with overhead valves. The redesigned engine boasted a shorter stroke and bigger bore, resulting in more power from the same 883-cc displacement. It was the start of a long and proud lineage. (Photograph © Andrew Morland)

shk-shk of sprinklers at dusk. On rare occasions, obviously lost on those streets lined with large Tudor homes harboring large station wagons and Lincoln Continentals in their Tudor garages, a motorcycle would rip the summer quiet. I would feel a sudden little annoyance in my small soul, already proprietary and judgmental; how odd, what an accidental gift, to grow up and one day walk through an unmarked door and find myself in the alternative universe of motorcycles and motorcyclists, where I would be shown, gently and with a patience I barely deserved, what a mistake I'd made.

I am a motorcyclist, and though I recognize I am not the "usual" motorcyclist, I also don't anticipate ever meeting one of those in person. All I know is that over the years I have occasionally sat back and thought how strange it is that motorcycles can completely overtake your being and act as if they own it. Certainly nothing in my life before them—and certainly not my parents, whose own interests run to chamber music, books, gardening, art, and cocktail parties—had prepared me to fall in love with bikes. I had gone through prep school, college, graduate school without knowing they existed. Those years were filled with sequential or concurrent passions: horses, the Civil War, dogs, bicycling, photography, poetry, the dream of true socialism, literary theory, and a couple dozen boys. I am still interested in all those things to some extent, except for the boyfriends, whose names I have largely forgotten, but the desire I came to feel for bikes eclipsed all of them, even though I still dream of having a horse.

Of all the things that could have happened to that girl when she grew up, motorcycles are fairly far down on the imaginable list. But now I can't imagine it otherwise. The whole thing reminds me of the story my father tells of when he was presented by his uncle with an awkwardly wrapped present; a metal point protruded from the top of the package. With a challenging swagger, Uncle Harold said, "Bet you can't guess what this is!"

Since it was utterly impossible to tell, my father figured he'd come up with the most absurd thing he could. "Why, it's a statue of Don Quixote, and that's his lance!" he proclaimed.

Uncle Harold's face fell. "How did you know?" he asked in suspicious deflation.

"Joe and Aggie's"
Just another stop on the endless American highway. This oil-on-canvas painting was created by James "Kingneon" Guçwa.
(Painting © 1999/Courtesy of Leslie Levy Creative Art Licensing)

*"I'd rather be busted into the wind like a meteorite than just
become dust. God made us to live, not just exist."*
—Evel Knievel before the Snake River Canyon jump, 1974